Be Your Own Life Coach

Be Your Own Life Coach

Jeff Archer

Teach Yourself®

DISCLAIMER

You're solely responsible for the way you view and use the information in this book, and do so at your own risk. The author and publisher are not responsible in any way for any kind of injuries or health problems that might occur due to using this book or following the advice in it.

For UK order enquiries: please contact
Bookpoint Ltd, 130 Milton Park, Abingdon, Oxon OX14 4SB.
Telephone: +44 (0) 1235 827720. *Fax:* +44 (0) 1235 400454.
Lines are open 09.00–17.00, Monday to Saturday, with a 24-hour message answering service. Details about our titles and how to order are available at www.teachyourself.com

For USA order enquiries: please contact McGraw-Hill Customer Services, PO Box 545, Blacklick, OH 43004-0545, USA.
Telephone: 1-800-722-4726. *Fax:* 1-614-755-5645.

For Canada order enquiries: please contact McGraw-Hill Ryerson Ltd, 300 Water St, Whitby, Ontario L1N 9B6, Canada.
Telephone: 905 430 5000. *Fax:* 905 430 5020.

Long renowned as the authoritative source for self-guided learning – with more than 50 million copies sold worldwide – the **Teach Yourself** series includes over 500 titles in the fields of languages, crafts, hobbies, business, computing and education.

British Library Cataloguing in Publication Data: a catalogue record for this title is available from the British Library.

Library of Congress Catalog Card Number: on file.

First published in UK 1994 by Hodder Education,
part of Hachette UK, 338 Euston Road, London NW1 3BH.

First published in US 1994 by the McGraw-Hill Companies, Inc.

This edition published 2010.

Previously published as *Teach Yourself Life Coach.*

The **Teach Yourself** name is a registered trade mark of Hodder Headline.

Typeset by Macmillan Publishing Solutions.

Printed in Great Britain for Hodder Education, an Hachette UK company, 338 Euston Road, London NW1 3BH, by CPI Cox & Wyman, Reading, Berkshire RG1 8EX.

The publisher has used its best endeavours to ensure that the URLs for external websites referred to in this book are correct and active at the time of going to press. However, the publisher and the author have no responsibility for the websites and can make no guarantee that a site will remain live or that the content will remain relevant, decent or appropriate.

Hachette UK's policy is to use papers that are natural, renewable and recyclable products and made from wood grown in sustainable forests. The logging and manufacturing processes are expected to conform to the environmental regulations of the country of origin.

Impression number   10 9 8 7 6 5 4 3
Year   2014 2013 2012 2011 2010

Contents

Meet the author

Welcome to *Be Your Own Life Coach*!

Congratulations on reaching a point in your life where you've decided not to settle for the situation you currently find yourself in but instead to take responsibility for achieving everything you deserve.

For many people it can feel like an easy option to live a passive existence and play the hand that life deals them, but for others it's much more exciting to get actively involved in everything you do and take charge of living as you think you ought to and get what you want out of every single day.

Over the years I've worked as a coach to hundreds of people who come to me in precisely the situation you find yourself in now. They may not be particularly unhappy with the way things are but they feel deep within themselves that there could be more to their daily lives and they want to find out how to achieve a more fulfilled way of living. They may wish to improve their confidence, their relationship, their work or career and financial situation, or maybe their fitness and energy levels. One thing they all have in common is that they want to make changes and they want to make them quickly and that's where the help of a coach can be invaluable.

The role of a coach is to guide with purpose and the role of this book is exactly the same: to help you ask the right questions of yourself and discover the answers that move you towards being the person you know you can be. Coaching is a means to fast-track your development, so be diligent in exploring your thoughts, feelings and attitudes when prompted by the book and you'll find that you can be experiencing new and exciting results immediately.

This is your opportunity to make a difference with your life and to begin making that difference right away. You should feel excited at the prospect of what you're capable of. Taking charge is a liberating experience. If you feel slightly nervous, so much the better as this will help you take focused action where you may have resisted making changes in the past. Trust your instincts and be true to your heart's desires and you'll be amazed at what you can achieve.

By picking up this book you've already completed the hardest part of any project, getting started. Now all you need to do is enjoy your journey to upgrading your life and make the most of all the positive results that you achieve from this day forward.

Only got a minute?

Life coaching is all about taking responsibility for your life and everything in it. It is a positive forward-looking process designed to establish:

▶ where you are now

▶ where you'd like your life to be

▶ how you can move quickly towards making your desired life a reality.

Life coaching involves taking new approaches, trying out new ideas and doing things differently from how you've done them in the past. It requires new analysis and examination

of the way you operate with a view to

uncovering how you can employ simple skills

to be the best you can be and get exactly what

you want out of your life.

5 Only got five minutes?

As we proceed through life we fall into patterns of behaviour that generally serve to make our lives easier. We develop rituals and routines and familiar habits that mean we don't have to think about every single thing we do each day. Limitations can arise however when circumstances change but we don't change our thoughts or behaviours accordingly. There is a danger that if we don't grow, evolve and develop as life moves on around us, we may end up feeling that life is controlling us rather than the other way round.

Life coaching enables people to 'check in' with themselves and make sure the life they find themselves leading is the life they want to be leading. In a busy modern world it's easy to lose sight of things we once held as important as we become more concerned with what needs to be done rather than with what we want to be doing. Problems can arise when the gap that develops between the life we want to live and the life we find ourselves caught up in each day is too great.

Because we are all so busy, life can feel overwhelming and making changes can feel impossible. This is where life coaching will help by encouraging a calm, measured approach that allows a clear focus on what's going on, and what action needs to be taken to make positive change. This is achieved by exploring key areas:

▶ Life coaching highlights priority areas for change.
▶ Life coaching helps develop specific plans for quick progress.
▶ Life coaching encourages action.
▶ Life coaching provides accountability.

Life coaching is a process during which you ask yourself new questions, questions that you may not have even considered in the past, and you demand answers of yourself. By following tried and tested strategies and techniques you'll be able to change the way you think, act and feel in many important areas of your life. Life coaching encourages you to hold a mirror up to your current routines and helps create new options and opportunities where in the past there may have been only limitations.

Life coaching is an exciting challenge that is both liberating and fulfilling. The quest to uncover your true desires in life and to create an existence that inspires you every day brings enjoyment and a new-found confidence in your abilities to make things happen.

10 Only got ten minutes?

Life coaching works by focusing on step-by-step plans for change and success. Every strategy and technique is tailored to suit the personality of the person being coached and their specific priorities. The coaching process is different for each individual though there are some identifiable trends and features.

Planning

If we don't make plans for how we want life to go, we shouldn't be surprised if we feel it's not turning out as we thought it would. A life without a plan is like a journey without a destination or a route and, although there is some benefit to be had from just 'going with the flow' at times, too much doing and not enough planning often leads people into areas where they become unsatisfied. Life coaching encourages planning for different parts of the future – the short, medium and long term – as a guideline for you to measure how you are progressing and as a means for you to check regularly if things are still proceeding as you would like them to.

Balance

Too much of anything, even things perceived to be good for us, can be a bad thing in the long term if life is lacking in balance. A mother devoted to her family may be left feeling lost when her children grow up and finally leave home. A successful career may be thrown into chaos when the moment finally arrives to spend more time with the family only to find they've all moved on while you were out working all hours. We may feel as though it's difficult to 'have it all' but it is vital to establish what balance is right for you and then to follow through and maintain this balance over time. Life coaching will help you both to uncover the elements of balance in your life and to plan ways of making sure there is space for all areas in your routine.

Self-awareness

If you want something different to happen in the future, you need to know exactly what's going on right now and why you experience the results that you do. Life coaching uses a number of techniques to help you assess your actions, thoughts and behaviours in relation to the results you get in order that you can pinpoint where you can do things differently for greatest effect.

As we become more self-aware we are better able to make decisions. We understand more about what makes us tick, why we make certain choices and what we are aiming to achieve. This knowledge helps us focus on the areas that are important to our overall objectives and in many cases helps us to say no to situations that would only divert us from our true desires.

Change

One of the most valuable facets of life coaching is its ability to prompt change. Making the journey through the coaching experience enables people to make changes they would previously have thought impossible.

Confidence

Self-confidence is vital when it comes to success in life. It's a factor that can make a huge difference every single day. As such, it's an area that life coaching focuses on and addresses through consistent, unthreatening challenge and growth. Growing in confidence often requires pushing ourselves out of our comfort zone and life coaching can help us achieve this in a controlled and manageable fashion.

Confidence comes from how we look, how we feel, the decisions we make, the company we keep and the quality of how we spend our time. Life coaching encourages analysis and development in each of these areas, where necessary, to help develop rock solid confidence in ourselves and our approach to life.

Motivation

With the right motivation, anything is possible. Life coaching helps to uncover what really motivates us into action and why. With this knowledge and understanding the power of the mind can be properly channelled and your results will be amazing.

Life coaching is a collection of tools and techniques that, with a little effort, you can use to create the life you've always dreamed of.

About the author

Jeff Archer is a lifestyle coach and Director of Upgrade My Life, a coaching consultancy working with individuals and organizations to help them perform to the best of their abilities in everything they do.

Real life, real people

Here is some feedback from individuals who have been coached by Jeff and Upgrade My Life:

I contacted Upgrade My Life having met up with an old friend who I had hardly recognized from the previous meeting six months beforehand. She had been working with Upgrade My Life and not only had her shape and posture changed but also very strikingly her attitude towards herself had changed.

I was intrigued and met up with a coach for one session a week for the first month. As I have a busy life like a lot of people, it was quite a commitment, and to be honest I wasn't that sure about this self-improvement business. But having tried every other trend that had come on the market in the last 20 years I was prepared to give it a go. I also do not like the idea of being bullied into doing things so it was a great relief to work with my coach who uses such gentle persuasion you do not really realize its happening. So by some miracle, four months later I have given up smoking, I exercise on average twice a week, walk every day and, by keeping a food diary, I have stopped binge eating. Oh, and my shape has changed to the point where people really notice.

I have been able to deal with my everyday and my working life so much more effectively by applying techniques that my coach has suggested. It is difficult to convey the progress made in this area but it has been immense. Also I feel that I have done it, made the moves and never once have I felt that I have been told to do anything. Yet I know I would not have done it without my coach's encouragement and guidance. His approach is unique in that he really considers the whole person, so it's a mind and body approach and, what's more, it works!

Frances

I've moved up my career path and got myself a great pay rise plus commission for everything I work on, which I have to say, was definitely achieved with the help of your coaching! So I'm rather pleased.

Tanya

I'm more confident in my abilities.

Malcolm

I feel a real sense of progress, I feel energized.

Karen

I feel like I've turned a corner and things are much clearer now.

Sally

I have my new job and it's with a company I never thought I'd be able to work for. My dream job! Thank you for all your help.

Maria

An amazing experience that I'd recommend to anyone who WANTS to change. I think it's important to be at the right point in your life to be able to effectively take on this kind of plan. I was, and reaped the benefits because of it.

Will

I have amazed myself.

Sam

I just want to say thanks for the help and guidance throughout the programme. Timing for me was amazing and this really did help me at a particularly bad stage of my life. I'm a lot happier with life, and feel a lot happier in myself.

Andrea

My programme made me think more and action the things I already knew I had to do, and prioritize better. It has given me much more self-confidence and positivity.

Sara

I surprised myself with my ability to make this plan, and even more so with the facts that I've already put some of it into action. I feel physically better but, more importantly, I feel back in control.

Brian

Introduction

Welcome to the beginning of your new life! By picking up this book you already know that you want to take charge of your destiny, and you are now on the way to learning and understanding everything you need to live life to the full.

Be Your Own Life Coach is designed to help you make your life better in every way – to help you enrich your day-to-day existence and get the most out of everything you do. You only get one shot at life and there is nothing more vital than living to the peak of your potential for every moment of every day. The objective of these pages is to help you to get maximum value and enjoyment out of everything you decide is important to you. At the moment you know how good life is. What you don't know yet is how great it could be with a little research and some simple analysis of what you really want.

What is life coaching?

Life coaching is a series of processes and a variety of techniques that can be applied to your current situation to create a happier and more fulfilling way of being. It is about looking at your life in a different way and it is a personal process that works in different ways for different people. The common theme in all coaching relationships is that by following the processes and applying the techniques, you will evolve and reach a better place than the one where you began. Whatever life is like for you now, you can use this book and the techniques within it, to make it even better.

Coaching is an ongoing process, and it would be a brave person who claimed to have 'mastered' the art of life. One thing you can always guarantee is that your life is ever-changing, and you must be alert to how you keep up with this change and, ideally, stay one step ahead of the game. You are learning all the time and constantly evolving from one task, situation or role in life to another. What matters is that you equip yourself properly to evolve in the way that suits you best and keeps you content. This book is designed to help you do just that.

Be Your Own Life Coach will help you explore what you love in life and what works for you so that you can do more of it. It will also guide you through an exploration of any aspects of your life that you're not so happy with in order for you to begin working immediately on improving these areas. You will learn to live your life in a new way, continually reviewing your progress, assessing where you want to be, expanding the positives and reducing the negatives, making each day more successful and more enjoyable than the last. To help you do this, the book is full of easy-to-follow advice and easy-to-implement strategies for success.

> *The unexamined life is not worth living.*
>
> Socrates, Apology 38a

By asking yourself the questions and applying the techniques in the book, you will be on a journey to a new existence with new direction and new purpose. You will be in control of what you do and where you are headed. You need never wake up with any feeling of dread at what the day might hold for you. Rather, you'll be equipped to embrace every day with an optimistic outlook, safe in the knowledge that everything you do is by your choice, of your making, and directed towards a fulfilled existence for you and those around you.

How does coaching work?

The effectiveness of the coaching process lies in the questions that are raised. You are constantly asking questions, both of yourself and of others; it is important that you ask the right questions, and it is vital that you answer these questions honestly and use this information wisely.

This book will help you to uncover the most incisive questions for you to ask in order to get the answers that lead you to where you want to be in life. Each chapter will guide you through various exercises designed to keep you on the path of discovery and self-development.

Sometimes, it may not be the easiest thing in the world to dig around in certain areas of what you do, but it is well worth taking the time to do it. This curiosity and investigation is the key to your success. It is the crucial factor in determining a life of confidence and satisfaction compared with a life of compromise and frustration. And it's what most people avoid. Pushing your frustrations to the back of your mind to carry on as you are is not uncommon, and often works for the short term. Yet it's not a great long-term solution as buried frustrations may recur and can affect you to a greater degree each time you experience them. Taking the time to work through the exercises in the book and generate solutions to the things that cause you anxiety and distress will lead you to quick and positive results, and will be the beginning of a whole new approach. It will be the difference that makes the difference to your life. Embrace the process and engage in it fully. Give it your all and you will be amazed at what you are capable of.

The results you achieve will ultimately equip you with a toolbox of methods and strategies that you know work for you and that you can employ whenever and wherever you need them.

The purpose of the book

Life coaching is all about approaching challenges with the correct mindset. It is a forward-looking process that acknowledges how you got to where you are today but doesn't allow your past to control your future. *Be Your Own Life Coach* will help you to examine the details of the life you have right now in the context of what you'd like to change. However, there will be no apportioning of blame or making excuses that you simply can't change things because you haven't been able to in the past.

Working through the book is not about dwelling on any current dissatisfaction that you may have with life; rather it is about uncovering the most exciting ideas that you have for how you'd like to live your life and then taking the necessary steps to create a life that you love. Each chapter will help you to focus on what you want most and will guide you progressively to a greater understanding of how you can think and behave differently to achieve the results that you always knew you were capable of but just haven't quite managed to put into practice yet.

Part one of the book explores how you see the world, how you choose to live, how you can set about making the changes that you'd like to make in your life and how you can best prepare yourself to become everything you've always wanted to be.

Part two builds on your new knowledge and positive mindset to show you how you can live the life you aspire to each and every day. This section examines how coaching strategies can be applied to various areas of life so that you can learn to use your new skills to maximum effect in a variety of different circumstances.

By the end of the book, you will be fully equipped to deal with any challenge that comes your way. The themes you will cover include the following:

A BRIGHTER FUTURE – GETTING STARTED

Chapter 1 helps you to examine what makes you happy and looks at how you can quickly begin to do more of these things in your life and less of the things that you don't enjoy so much. You will also learn how to shape your thoughts to implement changes guaranteed to help you get the most out of every day.

HOW ARE YOU DOING? EXAMINING THE
BIGGER PICTURE

In Chapter 2 you will learn to assess your life as a whole,
appreciate what's working, and pinpoint your priorities for
change. There is a guide to the process of breaking down your
challenges and establishing exactly what you need to think and
do in each area of life to reach your desired situation.

KNOW YOUR OWN MIND

Chapter 3 looks at what motivates you to action and will help you
to write your own personal mission statement. By examining your
values and your beliefs in life, you'll be in a strong position to act
in accordance with these fundamental aspects of your personality,
making you an unstoppable force to be reckoned with.

PLANNING YOUR LIFE

It's up to you to decide how your life is going to be in the future.
Chapter 4 teaches you how best to set out exactly what you want
to happen, and create the right mindset for success. The keys to
your success are within yourself and in the world around you.
You will learn how to tap into these resources for quick results.

THE BUSINESS OF LIFE – GETTING THE MOST
OUT OF EVERYTHING YOU DO

Chapter 5 looks at how to implement new approaches to help you
perform more efficiently on a day-to-day basis and to get more out
of what you choose to occupy yourself with as part of your regular
routine. Learn to be master of your own destiny and engage fully in
everything you do.

LOOKING GREAT, FEELING CONFIDENT

Do you pay enough attention to how you present yourself?
In Chapter 6 you will learn how to look and feel your best, make

a great impression everywhere you go, and feel brimming with confidence in every situation.

BEAUTIFUL BODY, ENDLESS ENERGY

In Chapter 7 you will discover how to settle on a plan of fitness and eating that really works for you and gets you the results you've always wanted. Forget diets and New Year's resolutions; this chapter will show you once and for all how to get the body and the energy you need for life.

SHAPE UP YOUR FINANCES

Do you have enough money? Do you know how much would be enough? Chapter 8 will help you work out how much you want, and show you strategies to make sure you get it. You will learn simple strategies to save money, to increase your earning power, and to think about what you'll do with your life when you achieve financial security and end your money worries once and for all.

FANTASTIC RELATIONSHIPS

Your relationships with those around you are crucial to your success and enjoyment of life. Chapter 9 looks at who you choose to spend time with, how you interact with others, and the effects these relationships have on you. There are a number of strategies to help you develop great relationships with everyone you come across.

THE NEW YOU – REAPING THE REWARDS

Having upgraded every area of your life, it is time that you celebrated your success. Chapter 10 encourages you to recognize how far you have come, appreciate your own triumphs, and motivate yourself for further success in the future.

SEVEN EASY STEPS TO SUCCESS

Each chapter includes a simple seven-step plan to help you put new strategies into action immediately. By acting on these seven steps, you will see just how easy it is to make changes and positively influence the way your life runs.

The approach

I have been working as a coach for a number of years now, and I love and believe in the techniques because I've tried them and made great changes to my life and the lives of hundreds of satisfied clients.

I first became interested in coaching through working in the fitness industry. Every day I worked with people who wanted to change their lives by changing their bodies, being fitter, getting thinner and feeling stronger. All agreed that looking after themselves made a big difference to their outlook and their demeanour, but some had greater success than others, and I wondered why this was. One answer lay in the ability of people to take a step back from the hustle and bustle of their everyday routine and find a balance in their lives that suited their every need – family, work and social – as well as taking care of their health and looking and feeling great. The most successful people struck the right balance that catered for all their needs and worked for them in the long term, enabling them to effectively achieve the objectives they set for themselves.

The next step for me was to find out how these people managed to create this balance. My interest in what makes people tick led me to research beyond the world of fitness and nutrition, and into the areas of lifestyle management, coaching and psychology. I wanted to explore the motives behind different behaviours and understand why people do what they do; I wanted to examine everything that goes into creating each person's life, success and happiness.

I set about using the information I learned from the people I worked with to identify successful strategies. Then I modified these strategies for others to show them how to break the mould of the current behaviours they were comfortable with but that weren't leading them to the results they desired.

I researched many self-help, personal development and coaching books, websites, training programmes and workshops to understand the different methods being used to teach people to get more out of their lives. Following this research, I developed an approach that is rooted in behaviour change, a willingness to experiment, and a desire to take prompt action. The approach also tackles the mind and the body together, allowing each to nourish the other. This book is an overview of the most common and most successful techniques applied to achieve dramatic change. The exercises have been developed by working with individuals who have achieved success and happiness, and there are many real-life case studies featured. You can use the experiences of others to lead you quickly to the self-knowledge that they may have spent months acquiring, and that you are now able to use to design your own template for success in everything you do.

Be Your Own Life Coach will enable you to fast-track yourself to the success you know you are capable of and the happiness that you fully deserve.

Quick tips for success

1 *Keep a notebook to accompany your thoughts as you read. You'll feel inspired as you learn things about yourself, and you'll come up with ideas beyond those covered in these pages. Use your notebook to jot down ingredients of your new life plan, and this will become an ongoing guidebook for your progress.*

2 *Have your diary close to hand. One of the keys to success is making a commitment to implement changes sooner rather than later. This process includes writing in a diary what you are going to do in order to reinforce your commitment to when you're going to do it. Successful people plan carefully*

what they are going to achieve and then, because they've planned carefully, they make sure these things happen.

3 *Your personal development is a lifelong project. Revisit the book regularly to ensure you are still on track with your objectives, to set yourself new targets, and to acknowledge the progress you have made so far. Different techniques will help you at different times, and continually applying the learning in the book to overcome successive challenges will keep you sharp and motivated.*

How this book will work for you

The book is designed to enable you to act as your own life coach when you need some extra guidance. The intention is not for you to be a life coach, but rather for you to be in a position to utilize some of the skills used in coaching to help you to move forward with your objectives.

Seven steps to success

1 IMMEDIATE ACTION

Write down everything that you'd like to be different in your life by the time you've finished this book. You might want to select some of the objectives from the list below and put a tick by each one that you'd like to achieve. Be sure to add plenty of your own objectives to your list.

By the time I finish working with this book I will:

- ▶ *feel in control of my destiny …*
- ▶ *feel less stressed …*
- ▶ *have better time management skills …*
- ▶ *be more effective at saying yes to what I want …*

- *be better at saying no to what I don't want …*
- *have greater enthusiasm for life …*
- *have more confidence …*
- *have more energy …*
- *feel my life is in balance …*
- *enjoy my life more …*
- *make the most of every opportunity …*
- *feel happier …*

Further personal objectives:

....
....
....
....
....

2 RING THE CHANGES

If you want things to be different, you'll need to think and act differently. Write down five ways in which you can be a different person today. For example, today I will be:

- *more assertive*
- *calmer*
- *healthier*
- *more confident*
- *more generous.*

Now write down five of your own. Today I will be:

1 ....
2 ....
3 ....
4 ....
5 ....

3 PLAN OF ATTACK

Decide where your opportunities are to put these changes into action
today. Perhaps you could plan to eat more healthily by buying a
healthy lunch on the way to work. Highlight your opportunities today;
perhaps you could behave more confidently in a meeting or briefing.
When will be a good time to act in a more generous fashion? What
can you do later to ensure you experience a period of calm today?

Today's opportunities for change:

....
....
....
....
....

4 PRIORITIZE

Of the changes that you want to make, decide what's most
important and put them in order. Tackle what's at the top first.

My desired changes as a priority list:

....
....
....
....
....

5 SAY YES

With your prioritized list in mind, say yes to everything that will
help you put these things into action. Do something every hour that
supports you in your objectives. If these actions are things that slightly
scare you, all the better. Get out of your comfort zone as often as you
can and it will become easier to live with greater challenges in your life.

6 SAY NO

With the prioritized list in mind, say no to everything that gets in the way of putting these things into action. Don't be rude, but be ruthless. To make quick changes, you need to put yourself higher up your priority list and make sure that your needs are catered for. Prioritize yourself properly and you will be in the best possible position for taking care of others.

7 BEGIN WITH THE END IN MIND

Decide, right now, how your life will be better by the end of this book if you are diligent about acting on your seven-step plan. If you make the changes you'd like to make, what does it mean for your day-to-day existence? Start thinking immediately about how you will feel and consider what others will be saying about you. What will you be wearing, what will you be thinking, how will you be acting and what will you be saying? Begin to create a mental picture of the new you that you are working towards, and then focus on it and refine and perfect it as often as you can.

Imagine sitting down to praise yourself at the end of the book. What achievements will you feel most proud of? What changes will give you the most satisfaction when you reflect back on them? Focus on all of your desires being achieved.

My greatest achievement will be:

....

My biggest change will be:

....

The greatest benefits of this book will be:

....

Part one

1

A brighter future – getting started

In this chapter you will learn:
- *what makes you happy*
- *how to do more of what you enjoy in life*
- *how to analyse your current behaviour*
- *the secrets of making successful changes.*

What makes you happy?

For generations, individuals have been searching to understand the meaning of life and have gone to the most amazing lengths to try to understand what it's all about and why we are here. Some travel to seek out new experiences and broaden the mind, and some crave isolation in the hope that introspection will lead them to the answers they are looking for.

However you choose to explore your existence, what is most important is that you choose to explore at all.

> *Curiosity is one of the permanent and certain characteristics of a vigorous intellect.*
>
> Samuel Johnson, *The Rambler*

Life is short and the world goes on without you when you're gone. What are you going to do to make a difference while you're here? What can you contribute? What is your mission in life?

There is a multitude of reasons why people do what they do. Examples of individual motivations include creating personal security, taking care of a family, being the best in a chosen field, helping others, creating a legacy that will outlive you and even just having fun.

Taking an overview of all the ideas that people perceive as crucial to their existence, the one common thread is that everyone wants to live as happily as they can.

Some contemporary surveys suggest that people who live in the developed world are currently at their unhappiest and that the general population was happier in the 1950s when, supposedly, life was simpler. If this is true, suggested reasons why people may feel unhappier than ever before are that they have much more freedom and many more options than ever before, and that the pressure to maximize these opportunities can lead individuals to struggle with what they are doing and what they think they should be doing. Perhaps they have too many options?

The truth of the matter is that today you are better equipped than ever to make changes in your life. The population is generally better off financially and better educated than previous generations, and has access to many more resources and information to help influence how they develop. The world moves at a fast pace and this can bring with it its own pressures. Time is precious, so quick and effective decision making is crucial. To help you make quick decisions, and make the correct decisions through life, you must first be clear about what makes you happy.

Happiness is rather intangible, but you know when you feel happy and you know when you're not happy. Research and experience show that people put more into life, and get more out of it, when they are able to do things they enjoy and that make them happy. It follows, then, that if you can establish the things that really make you happy and do more of them, you will instantly get more out of every day of your life.

> *Get as much happiness out of what you are doing as you can and don't put off being happy until some future date.*
>
> Dale Carnegie, author of *How to Win Friends and Influence People*

Insight

When you're considering what makes you happy, focus not only on instant gratification and what makes you happy today but consider also behaviours that have a longer-lasting impact and experiences that recur over time and make you happy on a regular basis.

Take a moment now to think about what makes you happy by asking yourself the following questions. Make a note of your answers.

▶ *When did I last feel truly happy?*
▶ *Where was I?*
▶ *What was I doing?*
▶ *Who was I with?*
▶ *What makes me happy on a regular basis?*
▶ *What activities make time fly for me?*

Think of as many times when you felt happy as you can. Now highlight the top five things in your life that are guaranteed to make you happy:

1
2
3
4
5

Real life, real people

Daniela was asked to list the top five things guaranteed to make her happy. Her response was:

1 Spending time with Ben and the children.
2 Running.
3 Reading.
4 Socializing.
5 Delivering successful presentations at work.

Now that you know what makes you happy, you must make sure that you do more of these things regularly. For each of the top five things that make you happy, make a note of the next time you will do each one of them. Use your diary or scheduler to help you plan accurately and to make sure you commit to each of the five things within the next 14 days. Plan a specific time for each commitment.

Today's date:

Date for next occurrence of each activity:

1
2
3
4
5

For Daniela, her commitments looked like this:

Today's date: Thursday 24 March

Date for next occurrence of each activity:

1 Sunday 27 March at 9.00 a.m. – spend time with husband and children.

2 Saturday 26 March at 7.30 a.m. – go running.
3 Tuesday 29 March at 9.30 p.m. – read.
4 Saturday 2 April at 8.00 p.m. – socialize.
5 Thursday 31 March 3.00 p.m. – deliver a successful presentation.

Now be as specific as you can with the details of the next occurrence of the five things that make you happy.

For each of your happiness activities, write down the details surrounding when it will be happening next. Where will you be, what will you be doing and, crucially, what do you need to put in place right now to make sure that each event takes place? What can you do today to guarantee you are able to do the things you enjoy?

Plan each happiness activity in detail

1
2
3
4
5

Daniela's detailed plan looked like this:

1 Spending time with Ben and the children

On Sunday the family will all be at home and I will arrange for some quality time for us all. Depending on how everyone is feeling we will either play together at home or visit the local park or swimming pool. To make sure nothing gets in the way of my plan, I will need to ensure that any domestic chores are completed by Saturday evening. I can do the supermarket shopping this evening and I can check in with my husband now to see what else needs doing so we can divide these tasks between us for completion on Saturday.

(Contd)

2 Going running

On Saturday I'll get up early so that I can go out for a run and be back in time for everyone else in the house getting up. I want to run for around an hour and be back in good time so I need to make sure that I have my kit ready the night before. Today I can pick a route that I like so that I can look forward to getting up and out.

3 Reading

Tuesday night is a quiet night in the house with no evening activities so we can eat at a sensible time and the kids can be in bed promptly. I can then tidy up the house and settle down in time for 9.30 p.m. Today I'll think about which book I'm going to read because picking something I know I'll really enjoy will ensure I protect my commitment to taking this time for me.

4 Socializing

On Saturday 2nd I will arrange for Ben and me to have dinner or drinks with friends. Over the next two or three days I will confirm where we will go. Today I need to make a couple of calls to find out who will be available for us to go out with. On Monday I will find a babysitter for the evening in question.

5 Delivering a successful presentation

Next Thursday I am making a presentation to 22 people in the office. I really want to do a good job and feel positive by the end of it. I know which room we'll be in and who will be attending so over the next few days I'll be thinking about everyone leaving the room, including me, having had a good experience and having achieved what we set out to achieve. I'm going to put together the content for the presentation by Monday evening and then practise it on Tuesday and Wednesday. Today I will devise a plan for putting the presentation together, and allocate time slots for working on it.

Taking charge – it's all in the planning

This may seem like a heavy-handed and somewhat deliberate process just to do a few things that you like doing, but when you try it you will understand how this approach works. Generally, the reason people don't do enough of what they like is that they don't plan these activities properly. They have their daily routine but these routines often don't contain enough of what brings them pleasure. The problem is that these routines can become deeply embedded and, in many cases, are perpetuated unconsciously if people do much that makes them unhappy without properly engaging with what they are doing or working out how they could make things better. They simply follow their familiar routine and hope they might have time for something enjoyable along the way.

Sometimes, people feel they can't do more of what they enjoy due to the pressures of everyday life and circumstances being beyond their control. They can feel dissatisfied, but don't spend the necessary time and effort focusing on what could be different. They tend to follow unconscious patterns of behaviour because these patterns don't require much thought. Problems arise when these familiar patterns can eventually make people frustrated and miserable.

To change the situation, you need to bring your patterns of behaviour into conscious thought. You need to examine and analyse what you do, what isn't working for you, and question what behaviour patterns might be more beneficial. Working through the above process does just that. It makes new strategies conscious, so that you know precisely what you must do in order to make life different and more fulfilling. The most exciting advantage of this process is that, by examining what's not working, making a conscious effort to establish new approaches and behaviour patterns and then putting them into action, you practise what works until this becomes your unconscious behaviour. You can return to not having to think so deeply about everything you do because you are now following new and positive unconscious behaviour patterns that get you what you want.

Doing more of the things that make you happy will instantly change your outlook on life. It will also leave you feeling more in control and positive, with the knowledge that you are running your life rather than feeling like the victim of circumstances. This will immediately reduce stress levels and increase your daily satisfaction.

Now and then it's good to pause in our pursuit of happiness and just be happy.

Guillaume Apollinaire, French poet and writer

YOUR PERSONAL PLAN FOR SUCCESS

Whatever you want in life, there are simple strategies for ensuring that your dreams become a reality. One quick system you can follow is to keep a daily journal to monitor specifically what happens in your life each day. Life is busy, and it is quite easy for your judgement to be clouded and for you to misrepresent what happens on any given day as you rush around from project to project – you are so preoccupied by getting things done that you overlook the very things you are actually achieving.

If you are looking to make changes in your life, you will want to make sure that you make the right changes. To make the most effective changes, you must know precisely what is going on with your life at the moment. By keeping a journal, you can track your progress by monitoring your current behaviour and the results you are getting. Then, if you need to modify your approach, you can very clearly see where the most effective changes can be made. Keeping a short personal journal is a great way to monitor what's working for you and what isn't. Look at how life is currently treating you by completing a journal entry for today.

Daily journal

Day/date:

What did I enjoy doing today?

What would I like to do more of?

What would I like to do less of?

What did I learn today?

What will I do differently tomorrow?

Thought for the day

Why keep a daily journal?
To make the most effective changes in your life, you must know
what's going on right now. You need to be aware of your current
thoughts and behaviours because it is precisely these thoughts and
behaviours that bring you the current results you are experiencing.
Once you make yourself consciously aware of the highs and lows
of each day, you can decide specifically what changes you'd like to
make so that you can increase the positive, decrease the negative,
and enhance your enjoyment of each successive 24 hours. The
questions in your daily journal will enable you to pinpoint what
you need to do and to take action quickly.

Insight
Record your daily journal information in a way that
makes it easy for you to make regular entries and is also
simple to refer back to. For some this may take the form
of a paper diary or hard copy journal, others prefer to
record things electronically on a computer, laptop or
portable device.

How does the daily journal work?

The daily journal works by placing everything you do in your conscious thoughts. It makes you aware of what makes up your daily routine and debunks any notions that 'life' is overwhelming by showing you which parts of your life are working well for you and which areas might not be satisfactory, while at the same time offering you the opportunity to come up with ways of improving your performance in these areas. Evolving your journal over time will ensure that the progress you make is ongoing. Looking back over your daily journals provides a great record of your positive development and also gives you information for future success. Each change you make or success you have is clearly recorded and can be modelled and reused in future.

WHAT DID I ENJOY DOING TODAY?

There will be some part of every day when you are enjoying yourself. Guaranteed. If you're lucky, you might have enjoyed the majority of the day. If it was a 'bad day', you may have to look a little harder for the enjoyment but it might be found in a conversation you had, a meeting you attended, time spent with your partner or family, or simply reading the paper on the way to work. Think about it and you'll be pleasantly surprised at what you come up with. Write down everything that you enjoyed today.

WHAT WOULD I LIKE TO DO MORE OF?

From the list of things you enjoyed, make a note of what you'd like more of in your life. If you can expand the positives sufficiently, there will no longer be room for any negatives.

WHAT WOULD I LIKE TO DO LESS OF?

Consider the parts of the day that you didn't enjoy so much. The purpose of this is not to dwell on the low points of each day but rather to begin the process of minimizing the frequency and the impact of these moments.

WHAT DID I LEARN TODAY?

It is vital that you keep learning as much as you can every single day. It is the quest for knowledge that will drive your life forward. It's natural for you to want to know more. Think about children and how curious they are. They never stop asking 'Why?' because their brains are like sponges and they want to understand everything. As they grow older, they can narrow their focus to specific things they are curious about and stop asking so many questions because they either don't have time or don't have the inclination to absorb so much information.

Examining what you learn each day will help you to appreciate that you do learn something every day and will also focus your attention on seeking out new experiences and new understanding. You have the capacity to continue learning, so choose to focus on learning what is most interesting and most beneficial to you. The more questions you ask, the keener your curiosity will become and the more you'll want to learn and learn and learn.

WHAT WILL I DO DIFFERENTLY TOMORROW?
There is a maxim in life coaching that 'there is no failure, only feedback'.

> *If you want to understand today, you have to search yesterday.*
>
> Pearl S. Buck, American novelist and Pulitzer Prize winner

There is also an acknowledgement that the definition of madness is to repeat the same activities, thoughts and behaviours and expect a different result. If you continue to do what you've always done, you'll always get what you've always got. To put it another way, if you want a different result in any area of your life, you have to change the way you behave and the way you think in this area.

Your frustration may be something as simple as often being late for work but still setting the alarm for the same time and hoping each day that you can get ready and get to the office on time. If the pattern has been repeated too many times without getting the right result, it's time to try something new. As with many of the techniques that make the difference, the things you are likely to do differently will be very straightforward ones such as setting the alarm ten minutes earlier or making a change to your morning routine that will allow you to get out of the house sooner. Use this section of your journal to begin a to-do list for the next day, and make sure that you keep this list regularly updated.

The details of the change you make are not the most important thing here, and the initial change may not be your final solution to a situation. What is important is being open-minded and prepared to try a different approach. It is amazing the amount of distress some people can cause themselves just because they won't change the habits of a lifetime. When you begin breaking old habits that don't work, you are on the road to finding the right solutions.

THOUGHT FOR THE DAY

One of the most powerful tools in the quest for changing your life is to change the way you think. The thought patterns that float through your mind every day are like familiar friends but, like some friends, they may not be that good for you. Your thoughts shape everything you do so it's important to be careful with what you're thinking. A successful strategy for positive thinking is to have a bank of ideas, affirmations and positive notions that you can refer to and that will always ensure you have an optimistic frame of mind.

Your thought, or thoughts, for the day can be ideas that you have had, comments that others have made that you found useful or inspiring, or quotations and excerpts from books, magazines, television programmes or films. Looking back over these thoughts every day will fill your mind with positivity leaving little or no room for negativity or doubt. There are examples of motivating quotations throughout this book. Think about how these words make you feel and collect a resource of as many words and thoughts that really inspire you as you can.

A journal success story – Jane

Jane is a mother of three who chose to take a six-month sabbatical from her work in a major British retailer. She had recently remarried and, although she was really enjoying her new relationship, she was still harbouring some negative emotion from the past and had been prescribed a course of anti-depressants by her doctor.

Jane was also experiencing some common symptoms of modern life. She often felt overwhelmed, experienced periods of self-doubt and was frequently harsh with her criticism of herself. She wanted to put her life in order, feel better about herself and increase her self-belief.

She decided that she would use the time away from work to put her negative emotions to bed and change the way she operated in time for her return to the office with a new perspective and a new attitude.

The first thing Jane did was begin a daily journal so that she could identify specific aspects of her behaviour that she was happy with, and highlight the finer details of what she wanted to change. She checked her journal twice a day – morning and night – and used the observations she made to compile a list of things to do and practical actions she could take towards her new persona. Keeping the journal and creating the to-do list instantly made her feel she was back in control of her life and that it was up to her what she thought and how she behaved. The satisfaction of ticking things off her to-do list also helped build Jane's confidence and her belief in herself that she was capable of taking charge and getting things done.

With her journal Jane planned everything that she had to do for herself and her family, allocated time slots for these activities and then put them into action. The benefits she felt were immense.

(Contd)

One thing that Jane knew would help her situation was setting clear boundaries for her family and devising a structure so that they all achieved their daily tasks and still had some time to have fun together. Her family is the most important thing to her but she felt she was missing out on quality time with them because the house was being run in a state of chaos. Setting out some details of each person's duties and then planning some activities together made a world of difference and has helped Jane to feel positive and satisfied with her role as a mother.

As Jane gained more control of her situation, she decided that one thing that would help her grow in confidence was if she were able to become more active and lose some weight. Initially she was unsure that she would be able to manage even a short walk more than twice a week but, with a bit of planning and some practical actions in the right direction, two months later she was going to the gym three or four times a week for 60–90 minutes each time. And what's more, she was enjoying it.

At the time of writing, Jane is about to return to work and is overjoyed to be going back as a very different person from the one who left six months ago. When asked about the secret of her success she commented:

I just needed some guidance to get me started. Once I had settled upon a way of thinking that would work for me, I was diligent in sticking to it. I made my plans, set my limits, stuck to them and, bit by bit, I made progress, which gave me more and more motivation. My journal showed me where I was dodging the real issues, and taking responsibility for the fact that I'm the only one that could make the situation better was a big step for me, but as soon as I accepted this, I began to realize that I can make it work. I'd never really planned before but now I know how to come up with strategies that I'm comfortable with, focus on what I want and get on with it. I feel ready now to take on any challenge and my colleagues aren't going to know what's hit them when I get back to the office.

One change or many?

Once you begin to make positive changes, life feels better and you may feel motivated to change as much as you can, as soon as you can. One question that often arises when people are overhauling their life is 'How many things should I try to change at once?' The answer simply boils down to how quickly you want to progress towards your new life, and how comfortable you are with the pace of change. The sooner you can begin behaving in the way you want your life to be, the faster this behaviour will become a reality. Often people are capable of making as many changes simultaneously as they choose to, so don't be afraid to set your sights high with the pace of change. Just make sure you keep track of your progress with your journal and then adjust your approach as necessary to incorporate more or less change depending on your current life circumstances.

Insight

On selected days it's an interesting challenge to try to do as many things as possible in a different way as an experiment to challenge your regular routines and find out where you can be more effective.

HOW LONG DOES CHANGE TAKE?

Another frequently asked question is 'How long will it take me to change an area of my life?' For many changes, the answer is similar to that for the question 'How long is a piece of string?' Change can be immediate as you can usually take some form of action straightaway that will alter the results you experience. The sooner you take these actions, observe the results and modify your approach accordingly, the sooner a complete change can be effected.

One way to guarantee that change is immediate is to make a change in the way you think about a particular issue or area of life. Even if you can't take immediate action directed towards your desired change, altering the way you think and feel about a situation will always be the first step to ensuring that change happens.

YOUR GREATEST ASSET FOR CHANGE

This is a good time to formally introduce you to your most valuable asset in your quest for fulfilment. The most powerful ally you have is a source of inspiration that will never let you down – your unconscious or subconscious mind. This is the mysterious part of you that some people refer to as 'intuition', 'gut feeling' or a 'sixth sense'.

When you are busy with a task or a project, or even thinking about what to have for lunch, it is your conscious mind that is focusing on the issue at hand. You make a decision on what to think about, and you concentrate on it. You may come up with a solution right there and then, or you may not.

When you choose to focus on particular thoughts, your unconscious mind takes care of everything else that needs to be considered to keep you safe, healthy and happy. While you think of lunch, your unconscious mind controls your breathing, keeps you upright and prevents you from walking into walls on your way to the restaurant. Your unconscious mind is your own personal autopilot. It is the part of your brain that is processing information all the time, even though you may not be aware of it.

You can train your unconscious mind to work in particular ways, and you must be careful about how you choose to programme this part of your mind. The power of the unconscious mind is clearly demonstrated by tasks such as driving or travelling a familiar journey like your daily commute to work. When you learn to drive, you really have to concentrate on what you are doing as there are so many tasks to be remembered and a potentially high price to pay if you make a mistake. When you first start a job, you have to plan your journey to the office carefully making sure you use the most efficient route, get your timings right and are safe at all times. Both these tasks are carried out completely consciously when you begin them and require a high degree of concentration.

As you repeat these tasks, they become more familiar and you can afford to focus less on what you are doing until eventually you can perform them while concentrating on something else completely. At this point, your unconscious mind has taken charge of these tasks, leaving your conscious mind free to focus on what might be more important at the time. Amazingly, the power of the unconscious mind is so great that you can trust it with something as complex and as important as getting you safely from A to B. And if you come across something slightly amiss on one of your journeys – a road diversion or a station closure – you can be sure that your unconscious mind will raise the alarm and send a signal to engage your conscious mind to work out what you will do about this interruption to your regular routine.

Your unconscious mind is a powerful resource and one not to be wasted. It runs your body while you are busy thinking of more interesting things to do, and it filters and files information while you sleep. It interprets the most important things learned each day and commits them to the part of your memory where you can access the information most easily. It is your unconscious mind that gives you those 'eureka' moments when you are busy working on one topic and the answer to something completely different, maybe something that you've been struggling with for days, suddenly pops into your head as if from out of nowhere.

USING YOUR ASSETS

If your unconscious mind is such a powerful tool, what can you do to get the best out of it? Put simply, you tune into how your unconscious mind is already working for you and then you make it work harder. First of all, think about when your unconscious mind has worked for you in the past.

- ▶ *When was the last time you had a gut feeling on something or someone?*
- ▶ *Did you act in accordance with your gut feeling or did you go against it?*
- ▶ *How did the situation turn out?*

Your instincts can be strong, and are rooted in a very quick assessment of what's going on in any situation in relation to your life experiences, what's best for you right there and then, what keeps you safe and what helps you through each day. In each situation that you enter, your unconscious mind will assess what's going on in relation to the information you have given it, which is based on what your conscious priorities in life are. Once you point your unconscious mind in a given direction, it will pick up on opportunities to help you move in that direction and will filter out information that it deems to be irrelevant to your objectives. To act against your gut instinct can lead to frustration and often ends with those moments where you say 'I knew I shouldn't have done that' or 'I knew how this was going to turn out'. Well you probably did, and it was your unconscious mind that was telling you.

To make the best use of your unconscious mind, give it something to work with. When you know what makes you happy, focus on these things regularly, and your unconscious mind will lead you to opportunities to do more of these things. If you're struggling with a problem, give it to your unconscious mind to work out the answer. Do something other than dwell on the issue. Take your conscious mind elsewhere for a while and go for a walk, do some gardening or even sleep on it and you are more likely to come up with a successful solution than if you just sit there racking your brain and going around in circles.

Insight

Your life will deliver whatever you focus on so choose to focus on specifically what you want rather than on what you don't want. Too many people focus on negative outcomes and then are surprised when these become the reality.

PRACTICE MAKES PERFECT

Trusting your instincts can be a daunting prospect so practise regularly and begin with relatively low-risk decisions. Make the effort to go with your gut feeling on at least three decisions every day and monitor your results.

EFFECTIVE DECISION MAKING

There's nothing worse than feeling indecisive. In the worst cases, failing to make decisions can lead to complete paralysis and an inability to move forward with anything. Trust your gut instinct and you will avoid this situation completely. Go with what you feel is right at the time and take action accordingly. You'll soon know if the action taken wasn't completely the right thing to do, but you can easily make adjustments to your approach until you refine the perfect solution. The important thing is that making a decision, any decision, will overcome paralysis and move you forward immediately. You can then amend the direction you're headed in according to the feedback you receive from your initial decision.

A SIMPLE EXAMPLE OF CHANGE

Learning to drive is a great illustration of a change most people make to their lives and the thought processes they employ to make these changes. To begin with, you have the current situation and something in life you want to alter. You can't drive and, for whatever reason, you know that your life would be better if you were able to drive. Consequently, you form an objective – to learn to drive – and research how you can make this happen. You ask others, probably your parents first, how they learned to drive, and then you find out who you can learn to drive with, probably through recommendations from friends or research from directories. Once you've done your research, you take action by calling an instructor and booking an appointment for your first lesson. You attend your lessons and practise new skills until you feel confident enough to take your driving test.

Learning to drive illustrates four clear stages of change and highlights the changing roles of your conscious and unconscious mind as you develop new skills.

1 Unconscious incompetence
This is when you don't know what you don't know. You see cars around but you're unaware that you could be driving one. At this

point in your life, driving is something that other people do. You have no comprehension of what might be involved in learning to drive.

2 Conscious incompetence
This is when you know what you don't know. You realize that driving is an option for you, and quite an attractive one at that. You have highlighted a new skill that you want to learn and you investigate the necessary steps to mastering that skill.

3 Conscious competence
This is when you are very aware of what you do know. Having established what you needed to learn in order to be able to drive, you have learned the necessary skills and mastered the art, but you still really have to concentrate on every aspect of doing it.

4 Unconscious competence
This is when you are capable of doing something but don't have to consciously engage in doing it. At this point, driving becomes second nature and you don't have to think about every gear change and every move you make.

Mastering the art of driving also demonstrates key features of facilitating change. These are features that you need to be aware of if you want change in your life to be fast and effective. The key features can be summarized as follows:

KEY FACTORS FOR SUCCESSFUL CHANGE
- ▸ *A clear objective*
- ▸ *Research*
- ▸ *Action*
- ▸ *Accountability*
- ▸ *Structure*
- ▸ *Feedback, flexibility and modification*
- ▸ *The end point*
- ▸ *A clear benefit*

A clear objective
For guaranteed success, you must be able to state your objective accurately and concisely: 'I'm going to learn to

drive and I'd like to pass my test within the next six months.'

Research
Knowing what you are setting out to achieve enables you to research the means to achieve your objective. Find out how one learns to drive – the method – and then find out how you are going to learn to drive – the practicalities. This will include whom you have lessons with, whose car you use, how many lessons you will aim to have and how much practice you can do between lessons.

Action

> *If you want to conquer fear, don't sit home and think about it. Go out and get busy.*
>
> Dale Carnegie, author of *How to Win Friends and Influence People*

Successful change begins with action and continues with more action. Action makes you feel positive and in control. You begin with finding out the facts and putting your resources in place. You take your first driving lesson and then practise repeatedly. You plan a schedule for your theory study and then keep up to date with it.

Accountability
Sharing your objective with others increases your accountability to making it work out for you. The more friends, family and colleagues that you tell what you're up to, the greater incentive you have to make a good job of it. Getting others involved also provides you with a strong support network.

Structure
There must always be a structured plan for how you will get from where you are now to where you want to be. In this case, the structure of the plan must include the number of lessons you anticipate, the time this will take out of your schedule, the content of the theory study and a time allocation for this, and any other preparation you need to do for your test.

Feedback, flexibility and modification

> *What separates the winners from the losers is how a person reacts to each new twist of fate.*
>
> Donald Trump

Even the best-laid plans need an element of flexibility. You must continually monitor your progress and modify your approach where necessary. Your initial objective may be to take your test in June but, if you really need more practice with your parallel parking and reversing around a corner, you may need to modify your plan to allow yourself more time to practise and then take your test in July. Being flexible should never be seen as compromising on your plan, rather, you are simply being realistic about how to achieve your desired result at the right time based on your current circumstances and rate of progress.

The end point
Every objective must have an end point. You must know when you've been successful so that you can appreciate your achievement and begin forming new objectives. You'll know you've succeeded when you hear someone say the words 'I'm pleased to say you have passed your driving test.'

A clear benefit
To smooth the path through any change or challenge, there must be a clear benefit to the action. You must be absolutely clear on how what you will have achieved by making the change will improve your life and the life of others around you. The clear benefits of passing your driving test are freedom, flexibility and fun.
Make sure that every positive change you set out to make has an element of reward built into it. Making a change is reward in itself. Creating as many benefits as possible from making the change will definitely increase your likelihood of quick success.

Insight
Spend plenty of time planning the positive results of making change. If you can generate enough excitement around the personal benefits of change, altering your behaviour to achieve these benefits will be simple.

THE LEARNING CYCLE

So now you can see and understand the simple processes that your mind goes through when you want to make changes. You begin at the point where you are living your life without really being aware that something might need to change. Then you see or experience an event that triggers a desire to make a change. You focus specifically on the change you need to make, how you can effect that change, and you practise new approaches and ways of behaving until you have achieved a new way of being. At this point, you allow your new behaviour to drift into the realm of unconscious living, leaving you free to focus your mind on new challenges.

Seven steps to success – a brighter future

1 IMMEDIATE ACTION

Write down what you can do right now to feel happier. Things like:

▶ *smile*
▶ *laugh*
▶ *put on some music you know will make you feel good*
▶ *call someone who you enjoy talking to*
▶ *finish something that's outstanding.*

2 RING THE CHANGES

How do you need to behave today in order to make sure you feel happy? Use your daily journal to isolate exactly what you need to do. Select from the following or choose your own behaviour changes. Today I will…

▶ *be more patient*
▶ *be more purposeful*
▶ *not get frustrated*
▶ *focus on positive options*
▶ *be more decisive*

- *be more forgiving*
- *prioritize my needs.*

3 PLAN OF ATTACK

Once you have decided how you will behave differently, open your mind and recognize your opportunities to act. Resist your familiar behaviour patterns and go with what feels right at the time. Monitor your results.

4 PRIORITIZE

Decide what is most important in your quest to make you happy. Specify the changes you will make first, and make sure they fit all the criteria for the key factors for successful change. Begin to make the most important changes right now.

5 SAY YES

Say yes only to things that will make you happy.

6 SAY NO

Say no to everything that will get in the way of you being happy.

7 BEGIN WITH THE END IN MIND

Decide, right now, how you will ensure that you feel happier by the end of today. What do you need to achieve to guarantee a feeling of satisfaction? When you get to the end of the day, what will you be thinking, what will you be saying to yourself, what achievement of the day will please you most?

SUMMARY, PRACTICAL ACTIONS AND COMMITMENTS

Only you can take control of your future and your happiness. You must make it your business to know what makes you happy and to ensure that you have as many opportunities for happiness and fulfilment as possible in your life. Keep your daily journal in detail, and be clear on what needs to change. Then make the necessary changes in a fashion and at a pace that you are comfortable with. Monitor your progress and each triumph will bring rewards, enjoyment and the motivation to strive for new success.

Chapter 1 is about getting started. Now you know:

▶ *how to recognize the things that make you happy and why they make you happy*
▶ *how to plan to do more of the things that make you happy*
▶ *how to review and assess your current behaviour*
▶ *how to make changes where you want to make them.*

Your commitment to yourself is to never let things go that you aren't happy with. If something isn't sitting quite right, investigate why and establish what changes you need to make to create a situation you are happier with.

New you checklist

At the end of Chapter 1 you will be able to complete the following checklist.

Tick each statement when you are satisfied with your progress in this area:

You know what makes you happy. ☐
You know when you will next do these activities. ☐
You keep a daily journal. ☐
You know how to tune into your unconscious mind. ☐
You know how to facilitate change in your life. ☐

10 THINGS TO REMEMBER

1 *Your state of mind is entirely up to you.*

2 *Spend time doing what makes you happy.*

3 *Plan for what you want to happen.*

4 *Monitor what you think and do, and make changes if you want to achieve better results.*

5 *Learn something new every day.*

6 *Try something new every day.*

7 *Have fun experimenting with change.*

8 *Hone the abilities of your unconscious mind.*

9 *Be open-minded and flexible.*

10 *Determine the personal benefits of everything you do and use these to motivate you to great results.*

2

....

How are you doing?

In this chapter you will learn:
- *to analyse your outlook on life*
- *to assess what areas of your life currently work well for you*
- *to pinpoint the areas where you are not yet satisfied*
- *to establish the quickest ways to make progress in each area of your life.*

Examining the bigger picture

Already you will feel happier about your life and will have taken steps to make positive changes. Yet what do you do if you don't yet know precisely what it is that you'd like to change? You may feel that something in your life isn't quite right, but you're not sure what. If you suspect that you don't have quite the right balance in life, nagging doubts can gnaw away at the back of your mind and distract your focus. The best thing you can do in this situation is to isolate what's bothering you and address these areas as soon as you can. If you are not currently satisfied with your life then something is missing. Find out what's missing quickly and attend to it immediately.

You will have areas of your life where you are completely satisfied and you will have areas where you want to make changes. For those areas you'd like to change, success is dependent on doing things differently, whether this be thinking about a situation slightly differently or acting with new approaches. For speedy results, it is vital that you make the changes sooner rather than later. Continued inactivity can lead to feelings that a problem is growing and that you'll never make headway with it. When problems grow you may struggle to tackle them, leaving you with the impression that because you can't solve them or reach the ideal solution quickly, you're better off doing nothing at all. It's true with any issue that you may not find the optimum solution straightaway but also true to say that if you do nothing, you'll never find the solution – swift action is the key here.

Insight

If something is bothering you, do not ignore it. Problems and issues very rarely solve themselves, so take charge of situations whenever possible, get involved and find out what's really going on.

Solving issues can be a gradual process, and you must take the first step in the process as soon as you can. Don't be afraid to experiment with different approaches, simply make a start and if your first approach isn't the best one for you, the feedback you get from taking the first step will help you to modify your behaviour for the next step and lead you gradually to a solution that works for you.

Don't be concerned if you are struggling with the first step to take in tackling any single problem or issue. If you find yourself in this position, be content with taking any action. Even if it doesn't seem directly related to what you are trying to achieve, doing something proactive will make you feel better. Action of any description will also always lead you somewhere. You will discover new information, find new ways of looking at issues and uncover new options as long as you keep an open mind and are willing to experiment. It's vital that

you are prepared to get busy in any area of life and see what
you learn.

> *There are no mistakes, no coincidences. All events are*
> *blessings given to us to learn from.*
>
> Elisabeth Kubler-Ross,
> author of *On Death and Dying*

What works and what doesn't

If you are experiencing dissatisfaction but you don't really know
why, an extremely useful exercise is to take a look at various
aspects of your personality by examining your mindset and
outlook in all areas of your life.

Take a look at the questionnaire below and rate your satisfaction
in each of the areas. Scoring zero means you are completely
dissatisfied in this area. Scoring ten means you are completely
satisfied with this part of your life. The numbers in between
represent your current satisfaction level in each area.

A helpful tip for completing the questionnaire is to rate yourself
according to how happy you are with your current situation. Don't
compare yourself to your idea of the perfect fitness, relationship
or career; simply choose a score that reflects your satisfaction right
now in each area compared with your success in each area in the
past, or the progress you feel you are capable of in each area in
the future.

Insight

When scoring yourself out of ten for any area of life, make
quick judgements and go with your initial answer. Trust your
instincts and don't allow your conscious mind too much time
to cloud the water with emotional interference.

LIFESTYLE RATINGS QUESTIONNAIRE

	Dissatisfied										*Fully satisfied*
Confidence levels	0	1	2	3	4	5	6	7	8	9	10
Personal relationships	0	1	2	3	4	5	6	7	8	9	10
Family life	0	1	2	3	4	5	6	7	8	9	10
Friends	0	1	2	3	4	5	6	7	8	9	10
Effectiveness at home	0	1	2	3	4	5	6	7	8	9	10
Energy levels	0	1	2	3	4	5	6	7	8	9	10
Fitness	0	1	2	3	4	5	6	7	8	9	10
Stamina	0	1	2	3	4	5	6	7	8	9	10
Nutrition habits	0	1	2	3	4	5	6	7	8	9	10
Body shape	0	1	2	3	4	5	6	7	8	9	10
Physical appearance	0	1	2	3	4	5	6	7	8	9	10
Career development	0	1	2	3	4	5	6	7	8	9	10
Financial situation	0	1	2	3	4	5	6	7	8	9	10
Ability to cope with stress	0	1	2	3	4	5	6	7	8	9	10
Effectiveness at work	0	1	2	3	4	5	6	7	8	9	10
Enjoyment of your leisure time	0	1	2	3	4	5	6	7	8	9	10
Ability to manage your time	0	1	2	3	4	5	6	7	8	9	10
Ability to prioritize	0	1	2	3	4	5	6	7	8	9	10
Personal development	0	1	2	3	4	5	6	7	8	9	10
Ability to balance your life	0	1	2	3	4	5	6	7	8	9	10
Happiness	0	1	2	3	4	5	6	7	8	9	10
Overall satisfaction with life	0	1	2	3	4	5	6	7	8	9	10

Before you go any further, answer the following questions:

▶ *What did you learn by assessing different aspects of your life?*

▶ *Do your scores reflect a balanced outlook on life?*

▶ *Have you thought about your life as a collection of different areas before?*

▶ *What did you observe by completing the chart?*

▶ *Which areas are you most satisfied with?*

▶ *Which areas are you least satisfied with?*

On completing your scores, you may find that you are pleasantly surprised by the fact that you are able to score yourself high in many areas. You may also find that, on closer inspection, some areas may not be as bad as you had considered them to be. Looking at your life as a collection of different areas of interest is useful as it calls into question the idea that 'life' isn't working for you. With this process you can clearly see that much of life will be working for you and that, with a few changes in selected areas, you will rapidly feel more in control of your overall situation.

Insight

Examine the areas where you score yourself highest and work out how you achieve success in these areas. Then consider how you can employ your own success strategies in areas where you are scoring yourself low.

What's magical about the process is that, while it enables you to draw positives from the higher scores, you can also see the close relationship between some of the areas that you've scored low in. There will be common themes in these areas that can be addressed simultaneously with new thoughts, behaviours and actions – when you're thinking about what changes you'd like to make to your life, focus on the areas in which you've scored lowest to begin with. Improving your rating from four to eight in a selection of areas will bring you a greater feeling of success than improving any single score from nine to ten.

Take a look at where you've scored lowest and consider the following questions for each area in turn.

Instant progress questions

1   What would have to happen in this area of my life for me to be able to score myself higher?

2   What would I like my rating out of ten to be in this area?

3   By what date could I improve my rating in this area?

4   What's the first action I need to take to begin raising my score in this area of my life?

5   When can I take this first action?

Real life, real people

When Anna ran through this exercise – see below – she scored lowest on her ability to manage her time, with her initial score being two out of ten in this area. It was also clear that her low score in this area was having a large impact on how she was able to score herself in other areas. Because she wasn't great at managing her time, she had lower scores than she would have liked in the areas of effectiveness at work, personal relationship, nutrition habits and effectiveness at home. Without a proper strategy for time management, Anna never had time to complete all her work as she would like, socialize with friends, go on dates, eat properly or keep up with the running of her house.

Lifestyle ratings questionnaire – Anna

	Dissatisfied										Fully satisfied
Confidence levels	0 1 2 3 4 5 6 **7** 8 9 10
Personal relationships	0 1 2 **3** 4 5 6 7 8 9 10
Family life	0 1 2 3 4 **5** 6 7 8 9 10
Friends	0 1 2 3 **4** 5 6 7 8 9 10
Effectiveness at home	0 1 2 **3** 4 5 6 7 8 9 10
Energy levels	0 1 2 3 **4** 5 6 7 8 9 10
Fitness	0 1 2 3 4 **5** 6 7 8 9 10
Stamina	0 1 2 3 4 **5** 6 7 8 9 10
Nutrition habits	0 1 2 **3** 4 5 6 7 8 9 10
Body shape	0 1 2 3 **4** 5 6 7 8 9 10
Physical appearance	0 1 2 3 4 **5** 6 7 8 9 10
Career development	0 1 2 3 4 5 **6** 7 8 9 10
Financial situation	0 1 2 3 4 **5** 6 7 8 9 10
Ability to cope with stress	0 1 2 3 4 5 6 7 8 **9** 10
Effectiveness at work	0 1 2 3 4 **5** 6 7 8 9 10
Enjoyment of your leisure time	0 1 2 **3** 4 5 6 7 8 9 10
Ability to manage your time	0 1 **2** 3 4 5 6 7 8 9 10
Ability to prioritize	0 1 2 **3** 4 5 6 7 8 9 10
Personal development	0 1 2 3 4 5 **6** 7 8 9 10
Ability to balance your life	0 1 2 3 4 5 6 7 8 9 10
Happiness	0 1 2 3 4 5 **6** 7 8 9 10
Overall satisfaction with life	0 1 2 3 4 5 **6** 7 8 9 10

(Contd)

When Anna analysed what she could do to change the situation, her responses looked like this:

Instant progress questions
Ability to manage time. Current rating 2/10 as at 10 October.

1 What would have to happen in this area of my life for me to be able to score myself higher?

I need to feel in control of my time. Currently I always feel that I'm playing catch-up with myself and others. My to-do list seems to get longer rather than shorter and I generally feel frustrated by the end of the day. For me to give myself a high score in this area I need to feel that I am on top of everything I have to do and that I am working at a speed that allows me to be productive but also enables me to fit in the rest of my life outside of work. To feel I have made improvements in this area I need to stop procrastinating and getting distracted. I do know what I should be doing to use my time more constructively but I need to be better at getting on with things. I need to focus on more doing and less thinking or talking.

2 What would I like my rating out of ten to be in this area?

For the moment, I'd settle for 8/10. That way I'd feel that I'm really making progress and heading in the right direction.

3 By what date could I improve my rating in this area?

I'm giving myself until the end of the year to have made some headway in this area. New Year is always a busy time for me so I need to be better at managing my time in preparation for January.

4 What's the first action I need to take to begin raising my score in this area of my life?

I need to take some time each day to look at my schedule, update my to-do list, make realistic plans around what I can achieve for work each day and each week, and then spend some time looking at what else needs attending to, particularly my personal life and my eating habits. I don't think it needs to be lots of time each day, but a regular check-in with myself would do me the world of good.

5 When can I take this first action?
I'm going to set aside 30 minutes today at 5 p.m. for my first planning session. Then I'll know specifically what I need to get on with over the coming days and can then decide what order in which to tackle things. Then, I guess if I'm serious about it, I need to set aside some time every day for regular check-ins with myself. It'll definitely be easier for the long term to do this in the mornings so I'll begin this routine tomorrow at 8 a.m. Then I can have half an hour without interruptions and see how I get on.

Guaranteed success

To guarantee instant action and swift progress, complete the instant progress questions for each of the areas of life that are a priority for you to improve.

When Anna had analysed her satisfaction ratings and was on her way to addressing the area most in need of change – her ability to manage her time – she decided to spend ten minutes of her regular 30-minute planning session applying the instant progress formula to one of her other priorities. She chose to look at her nutrition habits because improvements in this area would also help her with her concerns around her body shape and her energy levels. Her thoughts on her rating for her nutrition habits and what she could do about them were as follows:

Instant progress questions
Nutrition habits. Current rating 3/10 as at 11 October.

1 What would have to happen in this area of my life for me to be able to score myself higher?

(Contd)

I need to eat healthily throughout the day. I know I need more variety in my diet and I must cut out biscuits during the day. I also need to cut down the amount of wine I have in the evenings.

2 What would I like my rating out of ten to be in this area?
In this area of my life I'm an all or nothing person and I need to be completely happy with my food routine. I need to aim for a 10/10 score, at least to begin with, to make me feel as though I'm doing the right thing.

3 By what date could I improve my rating in this area?
I must start today and I'll give myself a couple of weeks to be properly back on track. That would mean I need to know I'm making significant progress by 25 October.

4 What's the first action I need to take to begin raising my score in this area of my life?
Buy a healthy lunch for today. I also need to get something nice to drink for later instead of resorting to wine, which is my habit most evenings.

5 When can I take this first action?
In half an hour on my way to work.

The instant progress questions got Anna started on her way to improving her rating in this area, particularly by thinking about the immediate action she could take.

Once you have established the areas of life you most wish to improve in and have outlined what you need to do in order to increase your satisfaction rating, you can consolidate your ideas on how to make fast, effective progress by drawing on the key factors for successful change as outlined in Chapter 1. Remember to put sufficient detail in each step of the process.

Key factors for successful change

- ▶ A clear objective
- ▶ Research
- ▶ Action
- ▶ Accountability
- ▶ Structure
- ▶ Feedback, flexibility and modification
- ▶ The end point
- ▶ A clear benefit

When Anna looked at her objectives for her nutrition habits in relation to the key factors needed for successful change, this is what she came up with:

Anna's nutrition habits – current rating 3/10

Key factors for successful change
- ▶ A clear objective

What are you setting out to achieve?
I need to change the way I eat. At the moment I am so busy that I either skip meals or snack on whatever I can get my hands on most quickly. I know this isn't doing me any good but I can't seem to change my routine. I would like to have a more regular eating pattern that makes me feel energetic and that I am doing my body good rather than feeling like I'm feeding myself up with junk.

- ▶ Research

What do you need to know to achieve your objective?
I need to know what my options are by finding out what kinds of food I can eat instead of the quick snacks and familiar options that I currently go for.

(Contd)

▶ Action

What do you need to do?
I need to set aside some time to look on the internet, read some books and speak to some people in the know so that I can gather information on what choices are open to me. I also need to look at my schedule to see where I can grab some regular time for planning what I'm going to eat, and then plan time to shop for it and prepare it.

▶ Accountability

In addition to yourself, who are you going to make yourself responsible to?
This is tricky. Everyone I know seems to be on one kind of diet or another or have some sort of agenda around what they eat, and some of my friends can be a really bad influence on me. I don't want a 'diet' but rather a more natural way of eating that I can sustain. I might find it distracting if I pick the wrong person to go through this with. I think to begin with I will be accountable to my daily journal where I'll keep track of exactly what's going on and how I feel about it. I will also share my objectives with my sister as she is usually a good support with things like this.

▶ Structure

Outline the progressive sequence of your actions towards your objective.

1 *Start my food journal.*
2 *Buy a healthy lunch and something nice to drink in the evenings.*
3 *Plan my research time.*
4 *Restructure my day slightly to take account of the time I need to devote to this area.*
5 *Start shopping for the right food and preparing it ahead of time.*

▶ Feedback, flexibility and modification

Consider all the aspects of your plan that you don't have full control over. Consider some contingency plans to keep you on track towards your objective in the face of new events and learning.

If others have snacks in the office, I need to have a healthier option near by so that I can be social but don't have to eat the biscuits. I don't want to be drinking every evening but I find it really difficult not to drink when I go out with my friends. I'll be better off not drinking on the nights that I'm at home but I'll need to have a new strategy to keep my mind off the wine at around 7 p.m. when I usually get home and go straight to the fridge to pour a glass to unwind. I'll buy some nice juice to drink at this point and will also launch straight into some of the household tasks that I would normally leave and then struggle with a bit later in the evening.

▶ End point

How will you know when you've achieved success? Describe what your life is like at this point.

Success in this area for me will be the feeling that I am in charge of my food routine and that I eat what I know makes me feel good, and avoid the things that I know I don't really want and that make me feel sluggish and guilty. I will have a routine for my food and drink and will feel completely in control of it.

▶ A clear benefit

The benefit of achieving change in this area is that I will feel better and have improved energy and focus.

WHAT'S THE POINT OF ALL THIS?

You already know that your greatest power to succeed comes from the power of your unconscious mind. You have to decide how you are going to programme your mind so that it can focus on what you really want and come up with efficient solutions for you.

The questions that you have answered so far are designed to raise your awareness of what's really going on in your life and to help you to begin focusing your mind towards where you want to be and when you want to be there. With your conscious mind and your unconscious mind focused in the same direction, you will now see opportunities for success where you may have missed them in the past.

THE POWER OF PICTURES

Taking time to thoroughly plan your objectives gives your mind an opportunity to create and visualize your success. What you focus on is what you will get, so make a decision now to focus on solutions and positive results. Planning your success means you can create it mentally before you begin to live it for real. The more often you visualize success and the more detail you can create in your mental pictures, the quicker your triumphs will come to fruition.

Insight

As well as creating internal visions of your future success, collect images and visual prompts that you will see regularly each day that will remind you of your mission with upgrading your life.

CASE STUDY

Real life, real people

A change success story – Anna
After completing her lifestyle ratings questionnaire, Anna stuck religiously to keeping time aside for research and planning. This helped her to feel more in control of her time management, particularly at work where she got so organized that she managed to find time to look for a new job that she subsequently switched to and loves. Taking time to plan her food patterns resulted in Anna losing 9.5 kg (21 lb) over the course of a single year, and the boost in confidence this gave her was enormous.

Seven steps to success – examining the bigger picture

1 IMMEDIATE ACTION

If something is bothering you right now, give yourself a score out of ten for how happy you are with this issue or in the area of life that it relates to.

2 RING THE CHANGES

Establish what behaviour will bridge the gap between your current score and a score of ten out of ten.

3 PLAN OF ATTACK

Choose when to start acting in the way you wish to. Focus on making practical changes as soon as you possibly can.

4 BE RESPONSIBLE

Take charge of your own destiny. Don't blame others and don't let others lead you astray. When you've decided what you want, stick with it and don't get distracted.

5 BE SINGLE-MINDED

It's up to you whether you live a four out of ten or a ten out of ten life. Say yes to ten out of ten and do everything you can to live by this as a rule.

6 BE CONSISTENT

Make sure that you do something that makes you feel ten out of ten every single day. Get used to feeling effective and satisfied. Note everything down in your journal to create a body of evidence that you are able to live like this forever.

7 REVIEW REGULARLY

Get into the habit of using the lifestyle ratings questionnaire scale frequently. This enables you to appreciate when things are going well and you can award a high score. High ratings can usually be attributed to times when you are living in the moment and are totally focused on what you are doing. Be aware of when these times happen for you and seek out more of them. Reviewing your ratings regularly also sets your mind thinking of small changes that you can continually make to keep your satisfaction scores high.

SUMMARY, PRACTICAL ACTIONS AND COMMITMENTS

If you're not happy with something in your life, find out what it is that you're unhappy with and what you need to do about it, and then take immediate action.

Chapter 2 is all about action. Now you know:

▶ *what aspects of your life and your state of mind you are happy with*
▶ *where you'd really like to make changes*
▶ *what specific actions you need to implement in order to live your ten out of ten life.*

Your commitment to yourself now is to keep your eyes and ears open and to quickly put a stop to anything that threatens your ten out of ten lifestyle.

New you checklist

At the end of Chapter 2 you will be able to complete the following checklist.

Tick each statement when you are satisfied with your progress in this area:

You know how to assess your progress in all areas of life. ☐
You know how to pinpoint changes you'd like to make. ☐
You know how to put change into action. ☐
You understand the importance of immediate action. ☐
You know what ten out of ten satisfaction feels like. ☐

10 THINGS TO REMEMBER

1 *Tackle distractions right away.*

2 *Avoid inactivity always.*

3 *Assess your satisfaction levels regularly.*

4 *Monitor your life balance periodically.*

5 *Be honest with where you'd like to make improvements.*

6 *Be specific when planning change.*

7 *Take action quickly.*

8 *Build up momentum with positive changes.*

9 *Align your conscious and unconscious minds.*

10 *Visuaslize success regularly.*

Know your own mind

In this chapter you will learn:
- *how to create your personal mission statement*
- *to fully understand your motivations, beliefs and values*
- *to use your motivations, beliefs and values to your advantage*
- *to ensure your values and beliefs are up to date and support you in your quest for your ideal life.*

Establishing what you really want in life

You now have a much better idea of the specific areas of life in which you would like to make changes. The chances are that, deep down, you knew where these changes needed to be made; but now you know specifically how to move forward in each area, and you will have already made progress with your aims. A question that often arises when individuals have taken time to think a little more about what they want and need is 'Why did I never do this before?'

Insight

Too much time spent lamenting the past only serves to stifle your ability to enjoy the present and create an exciting future. Learn the lessons that got you to where you are now and use this information to create your brilliant future.

Much of the frustration of modern living stems from people making too much compromise on who they are and what they want. Those who live the most satisfying lives are the people who chase their dreams, live in accordance with what they value and follow what they believe in. In order for you to pursue this successful model, you must be clear on what motivates you. You must know your own mind and you must act accordingly. No one is going to make your life decisions for you, and hopefully you wouldn't want them to. However, often people are swayed in one direction or another that may not suit them best, simply because they are not clear enough or strong enough in their own conviction about what they need in their own lives.

To live to your full potential, you must investigate what you really want out of life and why what you want is important to you. Then you can properly define what it will mean to be truly successful on your own terms and you will be in the best possible position to put the necessary actions into place that will lead you to success.

The first part of the answer to the question 'Why did I never do this before?' is that in many cases people simply don't take the time to look closely enough at what needs to be done and what the first steps on the way to implementing change need to be.

The second, and perhaps more crucial, part of the answer is that possibly there haven't been compelling enough reasons to take the time to plan and make the necessary changes. If the idea of making changes to your life doesn't excite you enough, chances are that the upside of making these changes isn't yet big enough. Now that you know the areas to address and the actions to take, all you need is a good enough reason to put the changes into practice. Change for the sake of change is difficult to sustain, and making changes that someone else thinks would be good for you is an uphill struggle because your heart simply won't be in the task. To make successful changes and guarantee great results, you need to know what matters to you and why these things really matter. To help you clarify your thoughts in this area, take a look at the following questions:

Uncovering personal motivation 1 – what do you really want?

- ▶ If you could have anything in life, what would you have?

- ▶ If you were living your ideal life, what would you be doing
    - ▷ every day?
    - ▷ every week?
    - ▷ every month?
    - ▷ every year?

- ▶ What does success mean to you? Not to society or to your friends, family or those around you, but what does it mean to you? What would be your greatest success in life?

- ▶ What single thing would make you truly happy?

- ▶ If you were to live your life again, knowing what you know now, what would you do differently?

Too many times people get tied up doing what they think they ought to do or what their family or friends think they should be doing. They often get drawn into doing what they think society expects of them rather than focusing on what they would really like to be doing. The important thing for you to pay attention to right now is what you want and why you want these things.

What drives you?

Now you have some ideas of what you really want in life, it is important to pinpoint why you want these things and how you can best motivate yourself to achieve them. To help you do this, you must establish what currently motivates you, what drives you to success, and what gets you out of bed each day. What are your guiding lights, your mantras, the thoughts and dreams that flow through your head creating your personal choices and sustaining your mission in life?

> *The ones who want to achieve and win championships motivate themselves.*
>
> Mike Ditka, American football player and coach

Everyone is motivated by different factors. Why do you do the things you do? What lies beneath your thoughts, your behaviour, your actions and your relationships?

For the purpose of the next exercise, take a look back at your list of the things you enjoy doing from Chapter 1 (page 5) and answer the following questions:

Uncovering personal motivation 2 – why you want what you want

▶ Why do I enjoy doing these things?

▶ What does doing these things do for me or get for me?

▶ How does doing these things enhance my life?

(Contd)

> ▶ What's really important about doing these things in my life?

> ▶ How would I feel if I couldn't do these things in my life?

When you've answered the questions, you will have the information you need to put together a clear statement of why you do what you do. This statement can then be used to make decisions on what is important to you, what you will choose to do, and what you will choose not to do. This is an important step in living in a way that is completely in line with what you value most in life.

Real life, real people

CASE STUDY

As an example, let's return to Daniela. Her list of things that make her happy goes like this:

1 Spending time with my husband and children.
2 Running.
3 Reading.
4 Socializing.
5 Delivering successful presentations at work.

Here's how Daniela explored why she wanted to do more of these things:

Why do I enjoy doing these things?

CASE STUDY

Spending time with my family is the most important thing to me. I get great comfort and support from them and, although family life is busy and has its ups and downs, I really feel that this time enriches my life. It also makes me feel that I'm doing what I should be doing with my life which is looking after my children, taking care of them and equipping them for life.

I love running because I know that even if it might be the last thing I feel like doing sometimes, I always feel better when I get back. It helps me to clear my head and calm my mind and body.

I enjoy reading and socializing for similar reasons. Both make me feel like I'm learning from others and engaging with the wider world.

Presenting at work is enjoyable because I like the interaction with others in the company and I like the feeling of satisfaction each time a presentation is complete.

What does doing these things do for me or get for me?

The things I enjoy all make me feel alive and reassure me that I am progressing in life. I like a challenge, and all the things that make me happy challenge me in different ways. I like to be busy and want to feel that I'm always making the most of each day so I tend to look towards things that will keep my days varied and exciting. I like to push myself out of my comfort zone in different ways; socializing with different people does this to a certain extent and presenting at work really stretches me.

How does doing these things enhance my life?

I like to feel that my life will have some impact on those around me so the things that I like to do are usually directed towards this aim in some way. I like to look after my family, help out my friends and share knowledge with my work colleagues. Running and reading benefit me in a more personal way but both help me to relax and re-orientate myself, which in turn makes me happier and more effective at giving something back to those around me.

What's really important about doing these things in my life?

I think it's important to keep yourself and your life in some sort of context, and the things that make me happy are generally the
(Contd)

things that help me to understand how and where I fit in. Running and reading give me the opportunity to think and assess how I feel about my life. My family, my friends and my work all show me how I fit into the bigger picture. Knowing how I fit in helps me to decide how I want to develop for the future.

How would I feel if I couldn't do these things in my life?

If I couldn't do any of the things that make me happy I'd feel lost. I'd definitely feel unfulfilled as though I was just drifting through life rather than living with any sense of purpose. In a way I wouldn't feel as though I was living my life but just going through the motions and waiting until I could get around to doing the things I want to do.

When you analyse your behaviour this closely, it is easy to spot common themes which, when identified, can help to explain why some things are more enjoyable than others. This information is vital for future decision making.

Look at the key words and phrases contained in why Daniela enjoys her chosen activities. She talks about comfort, support and enriching her life. She also talks about learning, developing, challenging herself and the satisfaction of a job well done. Finally, interaction with others is clearly important to Daniela.

Your answers to this sequence of questions will help you to make quick decisions on what is important to you each day.

Insight

Get into the habit of engaging with what you think and say every day. Your thoughts and words can be very revealing of your own priorities and preoccupations and observing your language patterns can be very helpful in developing new approaches to life.

When you've identified the common themes in your answers, you are in a position to say yes to all the opportunities that are in keeping with these themes. Things that crop up in your life that are in conflict with what makes you happy should be treated with caution. Either you must seek to eliminate these incidents from your life or look to turn them to your advantage. Every time you come across one of these situations you must ask yourself, 'In this situation, where are the opportunities for me to live my life according to what matters most to me?'

A personal mission statement

Daniela used her findings to come up with a personal mission statement. A personal mission statement is a clear summary of why you do the things you do, and acts as a clear motivator to seek out new experiences that nourish your mission. Here's what Daniela wrote:

Daniela's mission statement

Every day I will seek out events, opportunities and activities that challenge me and help me to learn. My goal is to enrich my life and the lives of all those around me. I will endeavour to turn every situation in which I find myself into an opportunity to develop myself and others.

The final question in the personal motivation 2 sequence, 'How would I feel if I couldn't do these things in my life?' acts as a strong call to action. People often live without enough of what makes them happy for too long, but if you consider living without these things forever you will see the situation differently. If you're not prepared to get more of the things you enjoy into your life right now, when will you be? Beware the consequences of waiting until tomorrow to get started as tomorrow may never arrive. Make the choice – the life you want to live begins today, not tomorrow.

Your own mission statement will help you to stay on track with
what matters to you in life. Look back through your answers to the
questions on uncovering personal motivation in the previous section,
and summarize the key points in the form of your mission statement.

My mission statement

HOW TO MAKE SURE YOU LIVE BY YOUR MISSION STATEMENT EVERY DAY

Keep your mission statement close to hand at all times. Either
commit it to memory and repeat it regularly, or write it down and
make sure that you read it as often as you can. You can put as much
detail as you like into your mission statement, and it will evolve
over time. Keep it concise because living by a mission statement that
is short and to the point will simplify every decision you make.

THE VALUES OF A MISSION STATEMENT

A mission statement works because it is a short summary of what
you value in life and what matters to you. Looking at Daniela's
mission statement, her values can be summarized as challenge,
enrichment and development. Examples of core values that you may

hold dear are honesty, integrity, generosity and kindness. Everyone
has a value system, and being aware of your core values is a
sure-fire way to guarantee that you act in accordance with them at
all times. Knowing your core values explains how you feel in certain
situations. If what you do is in keeping with your value system,
you will feel content. If something goes against your values, you
will feel uncomfortable. If one of your key values is honesty and
someone lies to you or tries to persuade you to lie to someone else,
it's unlikely that you will go along with them. If you value being
thorough and your boss asks you to send out a report you've been
working on before you feel it is ready, you may resist this request.

If you feel uncomfortable in any situation, it's unlikely to be
an irrational feeling and more likely to be a case of your values
being challenged. Knowing this is what's happening helps you to
understand your discomfort.

If someone challenges your core values to an extent that you feel is
unacceptable, and you feel that to agree to a situation would lead
you to too much compromise, then you have a decision to make.
What can you do that will turn the situation around so that your
values are uncompromised and you can live by your mission
statement? Here, your mission statement comes into its own
because only when you have ensured that each situation allows you
to live by your mission statement will you be able to proceed
without reservation. Being absolutely clear on your current mission
statement will ensure that you never compromise your core values.

Insight

Common core values include honesty, integrity, loyalty,
respect, attention to detail, generosity, optimism, justice,
fairness, responsibility, punctuality and tolerance. It is useful
to know your own core values and the core values of others.

Use your mission statement and all the other information
you've learned about yourself so far to write down a list of
your core values.

The power of beliefs

What you believe determines how you behave, what you say and how you judge other people. It also determines the results you get in everything you do. If you believe that life is always going to be a struggle, it always will be. If you believe that relationships are hard work, chances are that every relationship you have will not be without problems.

FORMING BELIEFS

You will have heard the phrase 'Seeing is believing', which suggests that as soon as you have experienced something, you can believe it to be true. For example, if you witness an elderly man merrily driving along at 30 miles (48 km) per hour in a 60 mile (96 km) per hour zone with his hat on in the car, this might lead you to the belief that all people of a certain age who wear hats while driving are slow or bad drivers and a nuisance on the roads.

What do you believe in?

Make a list of things that you believe to be true in life. Examples of beliefs can be general: 'I believe the sun will rise in the morning', 'I believe that travel broadens the mind'; or they can be more personal: 'I believe that it is important to be in control', 'I believe it's important to practise what you preach', or 'I believe that one must always lead by example'.

Highlight five of your own beliefs:

1 I believe...

2 I believe...

3 I believe...

4 I believe...

5 I believe...

Seeing is not always believing.

Martin Luther King, Jr

In the world of coaching, the phrase 'Seeing is believing' is often turned on its head to read 'Believing is seeing'. In a way it doesn't matter how a belief came to be lodged in your head but the fact it is there will affect your life as your beliefs dictate what you choose to see. Every slow driver over the age of 55 with a hat on will reinforce the belief suggested on the previous page until it becomes unquestionable. The limitation here is that your beliefs can become so strong and fixed that you never question them beyond that moment. This may restrict your view of the world, leading to a situation where, because you rigidly believe that what you've decided is true is actually true, you may not even notice all the hat-wearing pensioners who drive well. Seeing what you want to see doesn't make things real anywhere other than in your head.

Your beliefs are usually generalizations designed to help you make sense of the world. Creating fixed beliefs is a way of saving yourself time and effort in the future. If you make a decision and create a belief, then you can hold that belief, meaning you won't have to make a judgement on every situation you come across. If you believe that all elderly drivers are bad drivers, you won't have to make a decision on every elderly driver you come across. You know they're bad drivers and you simply adjust your driving behaviour accordingly.

Similarly, the beliefs that you hold help you in your interaction with other people. If you hold particular beliefs, you are likely to surround yourself with people who hold similar beliefs. If you come across people who hold beliefs that are contrary to those you hold, you are less likely to invest time in them. Think about this now and complete the following exercises.

What beliefs do you hold that are common to those you are close to?

Name of friend/contact/associate   *Shared beliefs*

If you'd like to witness the power of beliefs in action, for one whole day keep a record of your interactions with other people and examine each in relation to your beliefs. Take account of everyone you come into contact with in person or on the telephone or email. Who do you engage with and why? What shared beliefs do you have with this group? Who did you give short shrift to? Why do you think you don't have patience with this group? It may be that all those people with whom you get on well share the belief that it is important to be on time. Other people whom you don't get on well with may all hold the belief that teamwork isn't important, it's what the individual does that counts. Think about how others fit into your belief system.

▶ *Whom did you get on well with today?*
▶ *How does this interaction relate to your beliefs?*
▶ *Whom did you not have so much time for?*
▶ *How does this relate to your beliefs?*

The above questions are useful as they help to explain some of the decisions and judgements that you make about people and situations throughout the day. They also highlight which of your beliefs you hold as the strongest because these will be the ones that appear most frequently as part of your decision-making processes.

As you familiarize yourself with your beliefs, you can see clearly how they shape your everyday life.

LIMITING BELIEFS

Understanding your beliefs in order to help guide you through life is a very useful process, but be aware that holding on to your beliefs too tightly could also lead to frustrations and limitations. If you believe that life is always going to be a struggle, this belief will loiter at the back of your mind and infiltrate everything you do. Getting up in the morning is difficult because your belief leads you to look for the parts of the day that will reinforce this thought process. Your brain will actively seek out the points at which each day could potentially be a struggle, hone in on these, and satisfy itself that you're right to hold this belief. You will see precisely the things that reinforce your belief and you will overlook any evidence to the contrary. If you believe that relationships are hard work, the mind has a tendency to highlight all the examples in any relationship that will confirm this. You see, and have confirmed, what you believe to be reality. But are these beliefs helpful to you? And how did they come to be formed in the first place?

It is sensible to assume that there is a positive intention in every thought or behaviour that you demonstrate. You would never set out to deliberately make life hard for yourself so there must have been a reason for you to form what might now, on closer inspection, turn out to be limiting or negative beliefs. Perhaps you grew up surrounded by people for whom life was a struggle, and you adopted this belief as it helped you to fit in and make sense of the world around you. Maybe you had one difficult relationship and, rather than repeat any of the distress this caused you, it's just easier to believe that relationships are hard work and that you're better off steering clear of them.

But what could you be missing out on? By living with a belief system that was formed for particular reasons, without ever questioning or updating it, you'll never know if these beliefs might be doing you more harm than good. Compare the following beliefs and consider how life might be different for the people who hold them.

Examining beliefs and choosing your thought patterns

a. Life is a struggle.
b. Life is full of challenges that will help me to grow.

a. Relationships are hard work.
b. Relationships have their ups and downs but anything that's worthwhile needs working at.

a. I find my job difficult.
b. I find my job challenging.

a. Money is tight.
b. Money is abundant.

a. I'll never be thin.
b. I could be thin if I chose to be.

What you believe is what you will see, so be very careful about what you choose to believe. Take the opportunity, right now, to update your belief system.

First, specify five beliefs that you hold that, on closer examination, may actually be limiting your progress in life.

1
2
3
4
5

Sheila did this exercise and this is what she came up with. These are long-held beliefs that Sheila concluded may be limiting her success:

1 Life is easier if you have more confidence, I believe I'm just not a confident person.
2 I've worked the long hours I work now for six years. I believe you need to work long hours to get everything done.
3 With careful budgeting you can avoid getting into debt. I believe it's important to earn just a bit more than you need to live on.
4 I believe it is important to be seen as a safe pair of hands.

Now look at where your beliefs may have come from, when were they developed and are they actually true? Sheila explored the same questions and here's what she discovered.

1 *Life is easier if you have more confidence, I believe I'm just not a confident person.*

Over a number of years at work, Sheila had arrived at the conclusion that she wasn't a confident person because she sometimes found it difficult to make her voice heard. At work she would often suggest new ideas that seemed to be ignored, only to find them acted upon soon afterwards when someone else suggested them. She felt that if she were a more confident character, she would be more dogged about making her points, which were obviously valuable ideas, and ensure that she got credit for them. This lack of confidence led Sheila to believe that she was just someone who was afraid to stand out from the crowd, and she eventually withdrew further and further away rather than putting herself forward with suggestions and ideas. She was convinced her lack of confidence would lead to her making a fool of herself.

Challenge the belief

To challenge this belief, Sheila considered whether there was an area of her life where she did feel confident. She loved to play golf

(Contd)

and it was while she was playing that she felt at her most relaxed. She had begun playing only relatively recently but had lowered her handicap considerably, won some tournaments at her local club, and had set herself the objective of being the best female golfer in the area. Hardly the behaviour and thoughts of someone lacking in confidence or afraid to stand out from the crowd.

Sheila could now see clearly that it wasn't true to say that she wasn't a confident person, just that she wasn't applying her confidence at work in the same way that she was elsewhere in life. This understanding helped Sheila to adopt a new approach at work. She created a new and more helpful belief: *I am a confident person who can achieve success. I believe that it's up to me to choose where I want to apply my confidence.*

2 *I've worked the long hours I work now for six years. I believe you need to work long hours to get everything done.*

Sheila's belief that you have to work long hours to get things done started when she took up her current role. Before she got promotion she worked shorter hours but her previous job had been less demanding. As the workload and the responsibility increased, so did the hours that Sheila dedicated to her role in order to get everything done. She reached a point where she no longer questioned the number of hours she spent at the office and, although she wasn't happy about it, she just got on with it.

Challenge the belief

Reviewing this belief allowed Sheila to consider what she was actually trying to achieve. Because she had become so used to the hours she spent working, she had never taken the opportunity to take a step back and consider that, although it is important to get the work done, this might not have to involve more and more work for her. Could there be other options on how the work gets done and are there any new systems or structures that would allow others to help out and give her some breathing space?

By believing that she had to work these long hours, Sheila was condemning herself to always working them. The long hours were clearly taking their toll and it was becoming more and more vital that an alternative way of working was established. Sheila created a new belief: *I believe that if a job takes up too many hours, you're not doing it in the most efficient way and it's therefore time to find a new way of doing it.*

By creating and reinforcing a belief that there was a way to get results without having to donate more of her own time, Sheila immediately opened up a whole host of opportunities to make her life easier.

3 *With careful budgeting you can avoid getting into debt. I believe it's important to earn just a bit more than you need to live on.*

Sheila had always been careful with money and as a result of this and her continued hard work, she had always earned enough money to cover her outgoings and keep herself comfortable. When she was growing up, her older brother got himself into debt and Sheila saw the pain and inconvenience this caused him and the rest of the family so she had always believed it to be crucial to stay out of debt.

Challenge the belief

Staying out of debt was one of Sheila's core beliefs but she also felt that recently, just being 'comfortable' wasn't enough for her anymore. To make sacrifices with her time and effort and to work as hard as she did was becoming more of a challenge, only to remain comfortable. As Sheila thought about it more she accepted that she had built up enough of a body of evidence to prove that she was unlikely to ever get into debt. She had never been in debt and her core belief around avoiding debt was unlikely to allow her to get anywhere close to a precarious financial situation. With this in mind she created a new belief around her earning which ran: *I know what matters when it comes to staying debt-free. I believe it's also important to seek out the maximum financial returns one can get for efforts put into work.*

(Contd)

This new belief is much more in line with the potential for Sheila to live a life of prosperity, enjoyment and reward rather than simply working to cover her costs.

4 *I believe it is important to be seen as a safe pair of hands.*

As Sheila was growing up, her family circumstances meant that she was often relied upon to help out the others and, in many cases, came to be viewed as the responsible one in the family who could be trusted to get things done. This led Sheila to continue this role through school and university and on into her work and her adult family life and social life.

Challenge the belief

Being a safe pair of hands had for years defined Sheila's role among those who knew her. Sheila found this to be somewhat of a burden as she had become soul mate, confidante and problem solver for too many people. This impacted heavily on her time and her own priorities and, ironically, the more people she tried to help, the less useful she could be for them as she found she was too tired to offer the best advice and was simply going through the motions. She decided to update her belief in this area to: *I believe that quality is better than quantity when it comes to helping others.*

Updating your beliefs

Write down five beliefs that you currently hold that may be limiting your success.

1
2
3
4
5

Challenge each of these beliefs to establish how these beliefs came to be formed. Think about the ways in which these specific beliefs may be limiting you. What are these beliefs costing you? If you didn't hold these beliefs, what might you be capable of?

1

2

3

4

5

Turn each limiting belief into a more positive belief.

1

2

3

4

5

Whatever you've chosen for your new beliefs, you must be certain that they serve a positive purpose for you. Your beliefs should be regularly investigated to ensure that they are up to date, based on current circumstances and relevant to your life as it is now. Beliefs should support you with your positive intentions for changing your life, and you must be able to state them with total confidence and certainty in order for you to achieve your greatest successes.

There are some examples of positive and supportive beliefs below. Look at the statements and read them aloud. Feel the control and liberation that comes with being able to state such beliefs out loud with unswerving certainty. Even if these examples are not completely relevant to your situation, you can imagine their effectiveness. Make sure you are as certain of your own current belief system.

Sample supportive beliefs

I believe with total certainty and without any shadow of doubt that I am capable of the career I want and the finances I deserve.

(Contd)

> I believe with total certainty and without any shadow of doubt that I will have a long and happy relationship.
>
> I believe with total certainty and without any shadow of doubt that I will reach my target weight and body shape.
>
> I believe with total certainty and without any shadow of doubt that I live a successful, happy and fulfilled life.

When you update your beliefs, you instruct your unconscious mind on how things are going to be from now on. You give it the opportunity to seek out new avenues and explore new ways of living within your updated belief system. Your unconscious mind likes clear instructions, so be explicit and be consistent with the thoughts that you have. Check your belief system regularly to ensure that you have total certainty and not a shadow of a doubt surrounding your beliefs and where they will lead you.

Insight

Check with yourself that there is no reason why you need to retain any of your lingering limiting self-beliefs and, if you can find no cause to perpetuate them, cast them off and replace them with empowering thoughts supported by positive actions.

Questioning long-established beliefs, challenging them and bringing them up to date removes any lingering doubts in your mind about what you are trying to achieve. Long-held or *negative* beliefs that go unchallenged can easily slow your progress with making changes in your life. Like a spring clean, by getting rid of outdated and negative beliefs, you'll be ridding yourself of old clutter that can distract you from what's important. Just as household clutter takes up valuable physical space, so mental clutter takes up valuable head space. Make sure you free up all your available brain power to get what you deserve in life rather than tripping yourself up with outdated and negative thoughts and beliefs.

Seven steps to success – know your own mind

1 IMMEDIATE ACTION

Ask yourself, right now, do my values and my belief system support me or distract me from complete success? Write down any out-of-date or negative or limiting beliefs that you may still have lingering in your mind.

2 RING THE CHANGES

Write down all your current values and beliefs that support and nourish your success in life.

3 PLAN OF ATTACK

Live by your core values every day. Repeat your positive beliefs morning, noon and night. Keep them written down until you know them by heart and can repeat them all regularly. At any time in your life, your updated values and belief system should be as solid as a rock. Your beliefs should be as firm and unquestionable as the fact that you know night follows day.

4 PRIORITIZE

Take regular action that is consistent with your values and beliefs. If a new belief is that you are a confident person, take regular confident action. If a new belief is that money is plentiful, go out and spend some on something nice for yourself or someone you know. If you believe you live a healthy life, make sure what you eat and drink and the activities you do are consistent with this.

5 REVIEW

As you live by your new values and beliefs, other values and beliefs will come to your notice. Where appropriate, adopt these and you will refine and perfect your belief system as time goes by.

Now that you're a confident person, you may also believe it's okay to speak up in meetings, to be noticed, to share your point of view, to earn what you're worth, and to go out and get what you want in life. Be aware each time your values and beliefs change or are updated. Think about how your life changes as your beliefs change. How does your behaviour change? How does the world look different?

6 PACK UP THE POSITIVES

Each time you update your belief system, acknowledge the fact that the old beliefs had a purpose and were created by you to fulfil a particular need at a particular time. Take the positives from each old belief and move on. Beliefs are like fashion trends and can be quick-changing. You might look back and wonder how you ever thought that holding a particular belief was a good idea. But, as with fashion, there are good reasons behind your beliefs at any time in your life. Having said that, you wouldn't dig out some out-of-fashion clothes for a new date or an important job interview, so don't take your outdated beliefs with you either.

7 CONTROL YOURSELF

Always question if what's in your head, right now, is helping or hindering your overall success. If it's hindering, work out what you can replace those thoughts with immediately. What might be a more useful value to hold? What is a more positive belief to live by? Your success will always be dictated by your mindset, so be a person who sees the glass as half full, every time.

SUMMARY, PRACTICAL ACTIONS AND COMMITMENTS

Self-knowledge is a powerful tool in moving your life in the direction in which you want it to go. By taking the time to create your mission statement and analyse your values and beliefs, you can set about running your life in a way that suits you and plays to your strengths. Understanding why you succeed in areas that are in keeping with your values and beliefs will help you to create similar success in other areas. By understanding what motivates you, what works for you, and why these things work, you can make quick decisions on every situation you find yourself in and use every circumstance to your advantage in reaching where you want to be.

Chapter 3 is about knowing yourself and understanding how to behave in a way that is consistent with your self-knowledge. Now you know:

▶ *how to create your personal mission statement*
▶ *how to pinpoint your values and use them to your advantage*
▶ *how to update your beliefs, overcome limiting beliefs and create a total belief system that supports you in your aims.*

Now your commitment to yourself is to keep your mission statement, your values and your beliefs up to date, and to live each day in a fashion that is consistent with all three.

New you checklist

At the end of Chapter 3 you will be able to complete the following checklist.

Tick each statement when you are satisfied with your progress in this area:

You can imagine your ideal life. ☐
You understand how to create a personal
mission statement. ☐
You understand your values in life. ☐
You understand your beliefs and how important
they are. ☐
You know how to overcome limiting beliefs. ☐
Your belief system is up to date and supportive
of your life and objectives. ☐

10 THINGS TO REMEMBER

1 *Only you can decide what you really want out of life.*

2 *Focus on the present and the future.*

3 *Compare your daily life with your ideal life, every day.*

4 *Understand what makes you happy.*

5 *Have a clear personal mission statement.*

6 *Live in accordance with your personal mission statement.*

7 *Know your personal values, update them and live by them.*

8 *Know your personal belief system, update it and live by it.*

9 *Never limit your own potential.*

10 *Monitor your thoughts, actions and behaviours at all times.*

4

Planning your life

In this chapter you will learn:
- *to take charge of and plan your own future*
- *to completely visualize success in your head before creating it in your life*
- *to create excellent reasons to make changes and uncover 'what's in it for you'*
- *to learn from others and model their success.*

It's up to you what happens next

There is a phrase that says it is important to 'have your own plan or you'll end up as part of someone else's plan'. Having taken the time and trouble to investigate your life and the way you operate, the next step is to use the information learned so far to create your long-term future. You now know the power of focusing on what you want in life and you have felt the benefits of taking active steps towards living the life you deserve. The fun really begins now as you decide how you are going to apply the new you for maximum results in the future.

You can now recognize the things that impede your progress in life. If you take on challenges that aren't in keeping with your mission statement, your progress may be slow. If you act in a way that conflicts with your beliefs and values, you may feel uncomfortable and compromised. Similarly, if you feel that you aren't making the desired progress through life, you will feel the frustration of your unfulfilled potential.

Michael was frustrated with his role at work. He had been in the same position for three-and-a-half years and, although there were many aspects of the role he still enjoyed, there were many parts of it that bored him. He felt slightly guilty with his own attitude that this work was 'beneath him', so the first stage in Michael's development was to appreciate that these sentiments are an integral part of how one naturally evolves through life. In fact, the parts of his job that he found boring were simply elements that he had mastered and perfected and could do without really thinking. His boredom was a sign that he was ready for a new challenge.

So what did Michael's future hold that would provide him with new challenges?

The sticking point for Michael was that he didn't know where to begin. He knew he wouldn't be able to stay motivated in his current role for much longer, but he just had no idea what would constitute a better alternative.

Purpose and desire

There is only one way to guarantee that you minimize any possible frustration in life, and that is to dictate your own plan for the way you want things to turn out. Creating your own agenda by setting goals or objectives will give you a sense of purpose and bring new meaning to everything you do. By setting well-defined objectives, you will quickly recognize all opportunities for reaching these objectives. Ensuring your objectives are in line with your mission statement, values and beliefs will speed your progress. Finding compelling reasons to fulfil these objectives will give you the desire and motivation needed to take firm, decisive and consistent action.

Nobody realizes that some people expend tremendous energy merely to be normal.

Albert Camus

GET EXCITED

Choose now not to be normal but to live a life that is extraordinary. Creating a future that excites you is of vital importance. If your future doesn't excite you, then why go to all the time and trouble of making things happen? Life is always going to be busy and you will always be challenged so make sure that you choose your challenges and make them the most inspiring you can imagine. Don't be satisfied with achieving the small stuff. Use all your achievements as a platform to let your mind wander and think big. The bigger the dream you create, the better the reality you will live.

Insight

Practise expanding your level of expectations by thinking carefully about what you want out of each day. Consider the results you'll achieve and then ask yourself how you could improve on this. What would be the next step forward? Continue this process until you begin to wonder if the bigger results are really possible. Chances are that they are possible and this is precisely what you should be aiming for.

The sooner you decide on what the future holds for you, the sooner you can begin working on all the circumstances that will lead to this future. By deciding when you want to achieve specific objectives, you will speed your progress along the way. Knowing where you are headed enables you to tune into all the opportunities that you come across on a daily basis that will help you to get there quickly. A clear sense of purpose will act in conjunction with your mission statement, values and beliefs to form your strategic decision-making process.

> *Expect the best, plan for the worst, and prepare to be surprised.*
>
> Denis Waitley, American author, speaker and peak performance expert

Focusing on the immediate future and the challenges of implementing change can create a sticking point to progress.

Thinking of the results you will achieve and the benefits these will bring is an instant motivator and will overcome any inertia you may experience. Making changes to your life can be surprisingly simple when you establish the benefits these changes will bring you.

> **Insight**
> Spend time writing up a list of benefits that you will experience by making change. These will be personal benefits and benefits to those around you. Make sure you have plenty of good reasons to make your desired changes or you'll slow your progress by finding plenty of reasons not to.

A common objection to setting new objectives and implementing change is that people perceive that they are stuck in their comfort zone. If this is the case, you should consider setting objectives that lead you to a zone that's even more comfortable than where you are now. Just because you are comfortable now doesn't mean that you always will be. Don't take chances, instead design your most comfortable future. Taking the time to outline how good things could be in the future often leads people to realize that their current comfort zone isn't actually that comfortable after all compared to what they could create with a bit of planning.

> **Top tip**
> As you go through life, always look for the personal upside of any situation or challenge. If you can work out what's in it for you, you will be well motivated to take action at all times.

Setting your objectives

Everyone has a different take on what constitutes short-, medium- and long-term planning, so for the following exercise you may want to adjust the time deadlines a little to suit the planning schedule that works best for you. Generally, short term should mean two to eight weeks, medium term six to twelve months and long term eighteen months and beyond.

Planner

Setting your objectives – what do you most want to achieve in life?

Today's date:

Work and career
▶ *4-week objectives*

▶ *6-month objectives*

▶ *18-month objectives*

Health, fitness, food, well-being
▶ *4-week objectives*

▶ *6-month objectives*

▶ *18-month objectives*

Hobbies, social, fun, relaxation
▶ *4-week objectives*

▶ *6-month objectives*

▶ *18-month objectives*

Partner, family and friends
▶ *4-week objectives*

▶ *6-month objectives*

▶ *18-month objectives*

(Contd)

Finances

▶ *4-week objectives*

▶ *6-month objectives*

▶ *18-month objectives*

As you know from the exercises you have already completed, the act of writing things down helps to formalize and refine your thought processes. Writing down your objectives in different areas of your life for different time frames will highlight the areas you want to work on most.

Insight

When thinking about the time frame in which you'd like to reach your chosen goals, be realistic. Give yourself enough time to experience results but make your deadline pressing enough to spur you into immediate action towards each goal.

Completing this exercise also shows whether or not you have plans for each area of life. If you find any area difficult to complete, chances are you'll be feeling a little adrift in this area. Now is the opportunity to pin down what you want to happen in these areas and when you want to see progress. This planning tool will show you how the balance of your life stacks up – are you planning for every area that's important to you and do you have plans for different time frames for each of these areas? It's important that you see progressive stages of development in each area with a balance between the areas at each time frame. This ensures you move forward in a controlled fashion.

You can have it all. You just can't have it all at one time.

Oprah Winfrey

Your planner will show you very clearly whether or not you might have too much on the agenda at any given time in the future. If this is the case you can shift items in the plan to suit your schedule better. It will also show you if you have too little on the agenda. This may sounds strange but it is often the case that too few challenges can be as dangerous as too many. The planner will show you if you have the correct level of challenge in different areas. You should aim to always feel challenged but never overwhelmed.

Insight

With practice you will come to understand the level of challenge that suits you best and allows you to grow and develop without feeling overwhelmed. When you know this you can make plans to ensure that you select the correct level of challenge during different periods of your life and you'll always feel as though you are in control.

The planner is an organic tool that must be reviewed regularly to monitor your progress – make sure you date it each time you review it and keep copies of previous planners. Your most successful strategies are also organic and you might not settle on the best solution for an issue straightaway. The planner will ensure that you stay on track with your overall objectives and will help you to modify your approaches accordingly.

Your planner will act in a similar way to your daily journal if reviewed regularly. You will see clearly how you are making progress and this will bring you a great sense of satisfaction and motivation for further success.

AN IMPORTANT REMINDER

You now have the self-knowledge and the skills to ensure that your planner looks exciting and contains ambitious plans for a great future. Don't settle for aiming for things that are just nice to have, aim for the things you really want in life.

Creating unstoppable momentum

Once you have your initial objectives on your planner, the next step is to find good reasons to guarantee that these objectives come to fruition. And this means really good reasons. Great reasons in fact. Reasons that turn your goals into something irresistible, something you absolutely have to make into a reality. The simplest way to achieve this is to visualize, in as much detail as possible, every aspect of achieving success.

Top tip
Many people accept their circumstances and make the best of them. Stand out from the crowd by planning the best possible set of circumstances for your life and then make them a reality.

Working through the following exercise will ensure that you have total clarity for all the positive reasons why reaching your goal is worthwhile for you. You must create the most vivid and exciting picture of your future that you are capable of and work on it until it is irresistible. You'll know your visualization is working when you can feel all the physical symptoms of excitement that go with living in the way that you are imagining. Continue to ask more questions of yourself and work on the answers that lead you to feel almost overwhelmed by the desire to make this dream a reality. Picture yourself living your dream life in all its detail. Keep working on the vision until it feels like you are living your future already. You can now use the powerful feelings generated by your visualization to take instant action towards creating a world around you that matches up to the mental images and physical feelings you have just experienced.

Visualizing success – what's in it for you?

When you reach your objective, how will you feel?
Confident? Self-satisfied? Triumphant? Powerful? Happy?

When you reach your objective, how will life be different? Imagine that you have just achieved your objective and consider how life now changes for you.

When you reach your objective, what does your day look like? What activities does your day contain?

When you reach your objective, what activities will you no longer have to put up with? Of the tasks on your current daily to-do lists, what will you be able to remove?

When you reach your objective, what will others be saying about you?

When you reach your objective, what do you say to others about yourself?

How does achieving your objective affect your self-image and the image you portray to those around you?

Is your vision of reaching your objective exciting enough to encourage you to take instant action?

What instant action will you take?

Visualizing your future gives you a distinct advantage in the quest for success as it prepares your mind for your great achievements to come. The sooner you imagine success, the sooner you will live it.

Top tips

When you have highlighted your objectives and visualized your success in detail, follow these three rules for quick success.

1 Take at least one action every day to bring your objective closer to reality. The action could be a phone call you make, a meeting you have or one that you arrange, an email you send, or something you write that moves you forward with your goal.

2 Create a new thought process every day. Challenge your values and beliefs and come up with a supportive thought for yourself for every single day. It might be that you take time to recognize your successes and write them down. See the glass as half full instead of half empty. Take note of where you see positives when in the past you may have only seen negatives. Choose to think that you can succeed. Challenge yourself to come up with solutions for every situation you find yourself in. Monitor the way you talk to yourself and avoid statements such as 'The problem here is…'. Think positive, think of solutions and think success at all times.

3 Adopt a new behaviour pattern to support your objectives every day. Spend five minutes each day planning and visualizing your success. Take some exercise each day to support your physical self. Eat regularly and well to ensure good health and positive energy. Arrive everywhere on time, always ensure you are well turned out, smile, and enjoy everything you do.

Commitment and motivation

When you have created your objectives and visualized them in as much detail as you can, ask yourself how committed you are to making these objectives a reality. For every goal that you really want in life, you will need a ten out of ten commitment level. It's true to say, and you will have noticed this with projects that you've taken on before, there is a direct correlation between your level of commitment and your level of results. If you approach a project with a five out of ten commitment level thinking, 'It'll be good if this works out so let's play it by ear and see how it goes', chances are you will achieve a five out of ten result.

If you really want to succeed, you need to approach your projects with complete commitment. If a job is worth doing, it is worth doing well, and if you really want to make a difference to how things will be in the future, you really need to focus your full attention on what you're aiming to achieve. Commitment creates motivation, motivation generates energy and energy leads to results.

If you rate your commitment for a project and find it to be less than ten out of ten, you must ask yourself what prevents you from feeling totally committed. What is it that is holding you up and blocking your progress? Pay attention to the answers here, as overcoming these issues can form mini objectives for your planner which, once achieved, will ensure success with your larger objectives. Treat your mini goals in the same way as you treat the larger goals. Set a deadline for achieving them, establish what you will gain by achieving these mini goals – what's in it for you – and then visualize success in every detail.

> *Losers live in the past. Winners learn from the past and enjoy working in the present toward the future.*
>
> Denis Waitley, American author, speaker and peak performance expert

Learning from others

When you have decided what you really want in life, you will begin to see the opportunities that move you closer to your objectives and you will act upon these opportunities quickly and efficiently. As you gain momentum with your progress in life, you will continually look for ways to move yourself forward more and more swiftly. The feelings of success that you experience are addictive and you will want to experience them as often as possible.

Learning your own lessons along the way is a crucial part of your development. There are also other techniques that you can employ to hasten your progress towards your ideal life.

For most of the things that you are setting out to achieve, it is highly likely that someone else will have done some of the work and paved the way for you. That's not to say that your objectives aren't original, simply that your ideas on how you want to create your life will have evolved from one external source or another. It is likely that you became aware of what others had achieved in their lives and this spurred you on to desire similar results for yourself. Consequently, you may not be the first to strive after particular objectives, but they are certainly original to you and your life.

The fact that someone else has paved the way for you is great news. You are now in a position where you can examine how they did what they did, model their success and quickly learn the lessons that may have taken them months or years to master. You don't need to worry about whether or not you will achieve success, or how you're going to achieve that success. All you need to concern yourself with is finding the correct person, or people, whose success you are going to copy, and then get down to work.

CHOOSING ROLE MODELS

Take a moment to think about it now and you will call to mind someone, or perhaps a selection of people, who share your ideals and seek to live by them. They might be people who are close to you, perhaps family, friends or colleagues, or individuals that you don't know so well, or maybe someone that you've only come across a couple of times but who made an impression on you. Alternatively, perhaps you can think of someone in the public eye who you admire because they think and act as you do or as you would like to.

By looking more closely at what it is you admire about these people and analysing how they behave, you can learn by their example and incorporate aspects of their positive behaviour into your own life.

Having role models in life is crucial to your success. If you don't have positive examples to follow, it can be hard to know precisely how to behave, particularly when moving out of your comfort zone. Following in the footsteps of someone you admire can really help to speed your progress towards your aims. You probably had role models and heroes when you were young but at some stage in your life you decided that you didn't need them any longer and that you were fine on your own.

Insight

As your life develops make sure that your role models are still appropriate. Be vigilant and look around for new role models all the time. Remember you're not looking to copy everything about your role models, just seeking to emulate what you consider to be their best attributes.

Following in the footsteps of others is a simple way to fast-track success. It's something everyone does instinctively from when they are very young: for example, when you were a baby and you saw adults walking, it looked like an interesting way of getting about, definitely more efficient than crawling, so you copied them, slowly but steadily, until you mastered the art.

Beginning to walk is a great example of how people learn when they are young, and clearly illustrates another point made earlier that there is no failure, only feedback. A child learning to walk will fall over hundreds of times. Even though she may hurt herself, she will continue to practise until she has mastered the task at hand. If children learning to walk gave up and thought they had failed after the first fall, their lives would be very different. But they don't. They persevere because they have a very clear objective to aim for – they know what it looks like to walk and they're not giving up until they've achieved it – and they have no concept of not making this objective a reality. They know they're going to be able to walk sooner or later so they just keep at it until they can. There is no doubt in their minds that they will be successful. They are totally committed to achieving their goal.

BE YOUR OWN ROLE MODEL

If you could harness this type of single-minded focus and dedication for the rest of your life, you'd be unstoppable, wouldn't you? Well, you had it once so chances are it will still be within you somewhere. Take a moment now to list three examples of times in the recent past when you were completely focused on an objective and didn't stop until you had achieved it. Choose anything from finishing a project at work to completing a sporting challenge – or even getting the shopping or housework done.

Three recent examples of when I was completely focused and effective

1
2
3

Now that you have evidence that you can achieve this state of being, what are the circumstances necessary for this to happen?

The circumstances surrounding my recent examples of when I was completely focused and effective

Circumstances may include things such as being well rested, having sufficient time, good preparation, clear objectives and the correct incentive.

1
2
3

Seek out the positive

The knowledge that you gain from running through these exercises is invaluable in creating the correct environment for success. Listing particular examples of when you were successful helps you to build up a body of evidence to show that you are capable of great achievements when you turn your mind fully to a task. Gathering evidence of your own successful strategies and circumstances also means that you can pinpoint very effectively when circumstances are not completely in your favour. You can then act promptly to alter situations where necessary to ensure that you are fully supported in your objectives and at the best advantage for the most positive result.

MODELLING YOUR OWN SUCCESSES

In the world today there seems to be a tendency for people to judge themselves very harshly. If something in their life isn't going according to plan, it can trigger a spiral of negative thoughts that leads them to conclude that they are incapable, ineffective, and not up to the job. If you ever find yourself falling into this trap, break the cycle of thought by thinking immediately about what you are good at. You are good at many things but will often overlook these things in your quest for complete perfection. Answer the questions in the previous activity and use your answers to plan a new approach in whatever area hasn't yet worked for you. If you have strategies that you know work for you in particular areas of your life, use them. There's no reason why they shouldn't work in other areas too.

Real life, real people

Hannah was a successful project manager in charge of large projects and a wide and varied team. At work it was vital that she was extremely organized and up to date with everything that was going on. Over the years, Hannah had developed a system where she managed information on each project at three different levels.

(Contd)

CASE STUDY

Level 1: A master spreadsheet with everyone involved, all tasks integral to the project and headline timings.

Level 2: A monthly planner.

Level 3: A weekly planner and daily to-do list.

Hannah lived by her 'bibles', as she called them, and never made a move without consulting them.

An area of her life where Hannah wasn't as successful as she would have liked was with her family. Because she was so busy with work, she often didn't get as much time as she wanted to spend with her parents and her sisters. When things were really bad, she would find herself unable to return phone calls and she would feel out of touch. Her frustration with the situation came to a head when she forgot to send her father a father's day card and gift.

Hannah's approach to how she managed her family was a world apart from the way she managed her daily life at work. It soon became apparent that she had created things this way with her family as a minor protest against her strict regime in the office. She felt that if she had to plan as religiously outside the office as she did within work time, her life would be governed by structure and wouldn't leave any time to just 'go with the flow'.

Hannah's difficulty was that her rebellion against structure outside the office led to dissatisfaction. She decided to model her successful approach at work and install some elements of these strategies in her private life. She began with a master spreadsheet on which she noted important events, birthdays, holidays and outings. She created a monthly planner that outlined how often she would like to see various members of her family, and enabled her to plan exactly when these visits would take place. She also compiled a weekly to-do list that included all calls she wanted to make to her family and a note of who was doing what and when they were doing it so that she could make her calls at the right time and ask the right questions of each person.

What Hannah discovered was that applying a little structure to this area of life kept her up to date with what everyone was doing and allowed her to really enjoy the time she spent with her family. Managing herself differently actually allowed her to relax and go with the flow when she was with her family in a way that she'd never managed before while she was constantly feeling guilty for not being as organized in this area as she thought she should be.

MODELLING THE SUCCESS OF OTHERS

Modelling your own success is a clever way to jump-start progress in any part of your life and it can be a very productive technique. Moreover, there's no need to stop there. Somewhere in the world there will be someone who has achieved everything that you want to achieve. All you need to do is seek them out. If these people are within your immediate circle of contact, talk to them and find out how they did it. Do not hesitate to grill them on the secrets of their success. People are generally flattered to be seen as an inspiration and are usually very happy to answer questions on themselves and their achievements. Listen to what they have to say and apply what's relevant to your own situation.

If you choose role models who are outside of your immediate circle, find ways of researching their achievements. Establish whether there is any way you can get closer to them to discover more. Read about them in magazines and newspapers or conduct your own research into their character and their approach online.

It's a good idea to have a number of role models for different areas of life and a couple of people whom you perceive as already living the life you aspire to. It could be their ambition, their lifestyle, their personality, their confidence or their general demeanour that attracts you to these people. Consider carefully what it is that they have that you would like more of in your life and pinpoint how you can make it happen.

List five people that you would like to use as role models and note down what it is about their character or their life that you admire and aspire to.

Role model 1
What is it about this person that inspires me?

Role model 2
What is it about this person that inspires me?

Role model 3
What is it about this person that inspires me?

Role model 4
What is it about this person that inspires me?

Role model 5
What is it about this person that inspires me?

Whatever it is about your role models that inspires you, you can create more of these character traits in your life by watching them closely. Study what it is that they do that creates the overall impression that attracts you towards them, and consider what elements you can add into your daily life. Select the best bits of each person's success and use these to design your own master strategies. Create your own new behaviours made up of a combination of the most attractive parts of your role models' success and an element of your own personality. You must be comfortable with these behaviours and you will be able to refine them using the feedback you get from trying them out. Select the situations where you try these behaviours and begin with changes that are a challenge but not too intimidating. As you become more comfortable with your new approaches, you will be able to apply them on a wider scale.

ACT AS IF

You already know how important it is to monitor your thoughts because they are crucial to determining your behaviour. Using your role models is a powerful way of developing your thought processes to support you in your aims through your behaviour. You might think that it's all very well in theory to model the behaviour of others, but you just don't think like they do so your behaviour may appear inconsistent. In coaching, there is a technique called 'act as if' which will help you to overcome this hesitation. It enables you to bridge the gap between theory and practice by acting as if you did think like these people. If you had the same mindset as your role models, how would you be able to act? Pretend that you have got the same mindset and act as if you are already in the place you want to be.

If you can't make it good, at least make it look good.

Bill Gates

If you don't think you are a confident person, act as if you were and consider how your behaviour and your thoughts would be different. If you don't think you are the right person to be promoted, act as if you are and monitor the new way you view your career. If you don't think you are someone who lives a healthy, fulfilled life, act as if you are this type of person. You will quickly highlight how you can behave differently and you can put this into action immediately.

You and whose army?

In today's chaotic world it's easy to feel that you have too much to do and too many people to answer to, and it can all become overwhelming. Sometimes, you may feel that it's you against the world and you've got no one on your side.

On occasions like this it's time to rally the troops. Instead of crumbling under the pressure, get instant help by calling up some positive thought patterns. Think about the examples of when you were completely focused and effective. What was it about those situations that was so successful for you? What can you draw from those situations and put into action immediately?

Now quickly think about how your role models would react if they were in your situation. What would they think about the issues you face and how would they navigate their way through them? Thinking about someone else dealing with a situation instantly takes the heat out of the moment for you and enables you to take a step back and see things with a little more clarity. By imagining what others would do, it allows you insight beyond what you might come up with by yourself. Use this insight in conjunction with your innermost feelings on what is right for you at the time and you will be in a great position to make the right decisions.

You're never on your own in any circumstances if you can generate an army of advisers in your head. Whether this advice comes from your own previous successes or your army of chosen role models, the route to success will be there for you whenever you need it.

> *Surround yourself with people most like the person you want to become. Stay away from anyone who can or will bring you down.*
>
> Tom Hopkins, sales trainer

YOUR CIRCLE OF INFLUENCE

Filling your life and your thoughts with positive role models will create the perfect mindset for success and now is the right time to make sure that everyone you associate with, in your life and in your mind, is a positive influence – people who give you inspiration to achieve your dreams, not people who sap your strength and hamper your ability to progress.

Spring clean your circle of influence

Make a note of everyone who plays a part in your life whom you would classify as positive influences: people who give you energy and inspiration and who help you succeed in life.

Note down everyone in your life who you feel is a negative influence: people who drain you of energy and slow your success.

Now highlight any new positive influences you can use to replace the negative influences.

Replacing negative influences may sound harsh, but you must consider how these people affect your performance. If they hold you back and have no contribution to make to your future, why do you want to associate with them?

Seven steps to success – planning your life

1 *IMMEDIATE ACTION*

Look at the plan for your future every day, check your objectives are all still relevant and make sure that you are doing something today that moves you closer to your objectives.

2 VISUALIZE

Remind yourself regularly of why your objectives are important to you. Build your exciting future in your mind and think about how this future benefits you as often as you can.

3 PLAN OF ATTACK

For all tasks that don't appear straightforward, apply successful strategies from other areas of your life. Consider how someone whom you admire might tackle these tasks.

4 SAY YES

Say yes to any external influences that move you forward in your aims. Say no to anyone and anything that will slow you down or lead you off track.

5 BE SINGLE-MINDED

You can create the life you want to live and you can put into action everything necessary to make this life your reality. Focus fully on your chosen objectives and tune in to all the opportunities that will take you there quickly.

6 BE CONSISTENT

Behave in a manner that is consistent with your objectives at all times. If you are clear on what you want out of life, others will recognize this and respond in a way that will help you achieve success.

7 REVIEW REGULARLY

The world is continually changing and you are always evolving and developing. Your objectives will change as you tick off various achievements, grow in confidence and change the shape of your life. Always check that your objectives are in line with your current state of development and appropriate to the world around you.

SUMMARY, PRACTICAL ACTIONS AND COMMITMENTS

In your life you have everything to play for. It's up to you to decide what you want to happen. If you want to make things different and better, there are no reasons to hesitate. Just because you are where you are now does not mean that you can't make changes. Your current situation is the result of choices made up until this point. You are fully capable of making choices from this point onwards that lead you towards everything that you've ever wanted. If you take the time to specify what you want in your life, decide when you want to have it, break your objectives down into a series of manageable challenges and focus on the biggest benefits to you of success, you will achieve all your dreams and desires. It's up to you to take charge and it's down to you to do it now. No one will do it for you and there will never be a better time to take control.

Chapter 4 is about creating your own future, making it exciting and fast-tracking your way towards your perfect life. Now you know:

▶ *the importance of planning your own development over the coming weeks, months and years*
▶ *how to make your future compelling and visualize the details of living your dream life*
▶ *how to learn from your own success and the success of others to uncover new approaches and hasten your progress in every area of life.*

Your commitment to yourself now is to make sure that you always take time to create your own future and to make it exciting. Do not simply aim for something better than what you have right now. Uncover what would be perfect in each area, what you really want to happen, and aim to make this a reality as soon as humanly possible.

New you checklist

At the end of Chapter 4 you will be able to complete the following checklist.

Tick each statement when you are satisfied with your progress in this area:

You understand the importance of setting objectives.	☐
You have a plan for all areas of your life.	☐
You can visualize your own success.	☐
You are fully committed to your success.	☐
You have a renewed sense of purpose.	☐
You have new role models to learn from.	☐
You understand how to 'act as if'.	☐

10 THINGS TO REMEMBER

1 *An exciting future is within your reach.*

2 *Focus on the benefits of everything you do.*

3 *Continually strive for improvement.*

4 *Plan your own destiny.*

5 *Review your progress regularly.*

6 *Live your dreams in your head first and then in reality.*

7 *Commit fully to what you really want.*

8 *Learn from others and emulate their success.*

9 *Utilize your own success strategies wherever you can.*

10 *Adopt successful approaches and practise them until you've mastered them.*

Part two

Part two of *Be Your Own Life Coach* focuses on continually coaching yourself to success every day, in every area of your life. There is little point going through life wishing you were a different person or wanting to do something different. At all times it is within your power to take charge and make changes that will alter the course of your day, your week and your life for the better.

Part one has shown you exactly how this is possible with a little thought, some key questions and some determined action. Part two contains many more techniques and strategies that you can call into action to increase the pace of your progress and to help you enjoy yourself along the way. Regardless of what stage of your development you have reached, if you always have the correct mindset and you know you are on the way to success, each day will bring with it a great sense of achievement and satisfaction.

Part two is all about learning to incorporate more new skills and simple strategies for success into your daily schedule. Clearly, the greatest success with change comes from adopting new approaches and refining them until you have a collection of strategies that you know is effective for what you are trying to achieve. The quicker you can experiment with these new approaches, the sooner you can perfect them. In part two there is a whole host of successful strategies researched and modelled from people who have used them and made them work.

The strategies outlined are flexible, and they cover different areas of life so that you can select your opportunities to put new thoughts and behaviours into action. You can apply the strategies to areas other than those in the examples given if you feel it more appropriate. For example, there may be some work strategies covered here that you feel would be better suited to your family life; or an approach to healthy living that you feel might benefit you more if you applied it to your finances. It's up to you to decide where and when you try out these new techniques; just make sure that you do try them in some form and use the feedback you experience to develop the strategies into the overall approach to coaching that suits you best.

How you choose to go about implementing change is also up to you. You could aim to try something new every day. You may try one strategy each week or you might prefer to tackle one area of your life for a set period, perhaps one week or one month, before moving on to the next. You can use the information in the previous chapters to help you to prioritize the areas you wish to work on first, and then you can get started.

5

The business of life – getting the most out of everything you do

In this chapter you will learn:
- *to apply coaching techniques at work and in your career*
- *to be master of your own destiny and engage fully in everything you do*
- *to structure your life so you are supported in every department*
- *to prioritize, delegate, multi-task and make the best use of your time*
- *how to achieve maximum value in everything you do.*

Do it, ditch it or delegate it

The world is moving fast, and as you live through each day, new challenges, tasks and issues will crop up. These will include opportunities to increase the pace of your progress, and useful new information and knowledge that will support your aims and objectives. There will also be issues that merely take up your valuable time, time that would be more usefully spent elsewhere. Now that you are clear on your personal objectives, following the mantra of 'do it, ditch it or delegate it' at all times will guarantee that you keep your focus where it needs to be. It will help you to decide quickly which opportunities are worth spending time and effort on. If something is relevant and supports you in your aims, do it. If something crops up that doesn't help you in your aims or is not relevant to your situation, remove it from your world. Things that are relevant to your aims and that can be managed or organized by someone else should be delegated, leaving you free to focus on your most vital priorities that only you can achieve.

> ### Insight
> Spend as much time as you can doing what you choose to do rather than reacting to events around you. The more you feel in control of your actions, the more effective these actions will be.

DO IT

There is a little flexibility here and this notion can be expanded slightly to 'either do it, right now, or make a plan of when you will definitely do it later in the day or the week'. This can apply to every single task that comes your way: opening the post, replying to emails, screening or answering phone calls, planning meetings or booking holidays. You must also qualify the 'do it', making it 'do it right and do it properly'. Attending to tasks half-heartedly only means you'll have to spend more time on them later on, and if you don't have time to do them properly now, what makes you think you'll have time to redo them later? If you can't do it properly, right now, pick a time later on when you will be able to.

This part of the process is great for helping you to clarify your priorities. If, for some reason, you don't manage to attend to the task immediately or at the appointed time, you now have to consider how much of a priority the task really is. Initially it may have appeared important but if it isn't enough of a priority to prompt you to action, perhaps it can be ditched or delegated.

DITCH IT

Here's an opportunity for you to practise being a little bit ruthless. If you're not going to take advantage of a 'once in a lifetime chance to save a fortune on your dream holiday' offer when it comes through your door or into your email in-box, you're probably not going to be interested in it later in the day or week, so throw it away right now. The same goes for all those 'interesting' emails that arrive on your computer every day, and incoming phone calls that you're not really interested in. Extra reading and research is great and all very well if you have time and if the reading matter is relevant. You can quickly read emails as they arrive if they are important, or you can file them to be read at a time you allocate for this kind of work, but don't get sidetracked reading about the latest developments in ball bearing technology or a brand new offer from a manufacturer of Wellington boots if you have more important things to think about. Remove these distractions immediately.

With telephone call interruptions, don't say you'll call the person back or, worse, ask them to call you back later. If you have time to deal with telephone issues, answer the call and deal with it. If you don't, manage your calls with your voicemail and either address each issue when you can focus on it properly or delete any unnecessarily distracting messages.

Top tip
At the end of each day, aim to keep your telephone message pad clear, your voicemail empty and your email in-box organized as an in-box rather than as an extended to-do list.

DELEGATE IT

When things crop up that are relevant to your aims, it doesn't necessarily follow that you have to be the one who follows a task through to completion. Considering what you can delegate is a useful exercise as it will show you how effective your systems, surroundings and support network are for achieving your objectives.

A common response to the notion of delegating is 'But I don't have anyone to delegate any of my tasks to. There's only me.' Well, just because there may only be you right now doesn't mean that it will always be this way. One thing is for sure though, if you insist on trying to do everything without any help along the way, you run the risk of limiting your growth and your potential. It will always be just you, and you have only one pair of hands so there's a chance you will always feel overstretched.

In every area of life it is important to plan for future growth. If you have a support network or a team of helpers in place already, use them wisely and leave yourself free to do the things that you enjoy most or the things that are most effectively done by you or even the things that only you can do. Get into the habit of delegating wherever possible and ensure that your team is equipped and trained for the tasks at hand.

> **Insight**
>
> If you find yourself resisting getting help with tasks, ask yourself why this might be. You may need to seek out new people and new resources but avoid ending up back at 'It's quicker if I just do it myself'. It might be quicker right now but you need to find ways to guarantee that you don't simply repeat the same jobs over and over again in the future.

Structure and hierarchy

If you don't yet have a team of people to whom you can delegate, start acting as though you do as this will help to add structure to the way you operate for the future. Imagine your life as a business. A strategic decision that every business must take at some point is whether to remain the same size or to grow – to continue operating as it is or to move forward to the next level. You will regularly face the same decision in different areas of your life and you will need to decide if you would like to perpetuate the status quo in these areas or develop them into something new. If the decision is to grow, then an organization must be built for growth with a leader, a clear direction, and a number of different departments all specializing in their own particular area. For your life to grow and redevelop you must create a similar supportive structure.

Your life structure

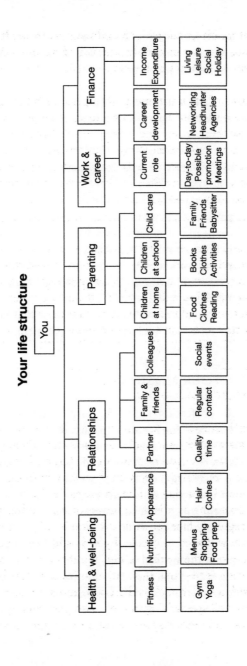

If you were to set your life out in the same way that an organization sets out its structure, what would it look like? Your department headings might look something like the chart on page 105.

> Use this life structure as a template and sketch out your personal operating structure. Add any other departments that are relevant to your life.

As you can see, the life structure can become quite extensive, but sketching an outline like this is very useful because it clearly demonstrates every aspect of your life that you are responsible for. Each department has an important role to play in your overall success and, as head of each department, you must dictate how each department is organized. Now that you can see the structure of your life in front of you, you can decide if you'd like it to remain as it is or if you would like it to develop. If you choose to develop your life, some changes will need to be made and, by looking at your structure, you can see what will need to be delegated, make some decisions on which area to act in first, and choose the speed of development in each area.

CHOOSE YOUR MISSION

To do a totally professional job, you must have the correct mindset and the right attitude for heading up each department of your life. As the leader of each department, it's up to you to write the mission statement for each area and choose what has to be achieved. Use what you have learned so far – your knowledge of your values and what really matters to you – to create a short mission statement for each department. The statements may run along the following lines:

> **Department: Health & well-being**
> **Mission:** To ensure I am physically fit and well and capable of achieving all the things I'd like to achieve. To look after and develop myself in order that I can be successful at what I do, live with a sense of purpose and fulfilment, and enjoy my life.

Now you can clearly see the departments of your life and what
each department needs to achieve. Whether you wish to grow
each department or operate each one at the existing level but in
a more efficient fashion, the next step is to create a tight structure
for every area.

Select one department and write out everything that needs to be
done within this department, in order to achieve its given objective.
This forms the basis of a 'job description' for each life area.

Department: Health & well-being
Tasks and objectives:
▶ Keep abreast of regular medical checks.
▶ Seek specialist advice when necessary.
▶ Plan and facilitate regular exercise.
▶ Attend regular yoga classes.
▶ Walk 10,000 steps each day.
▶ Plan healthy menus, meals and snacks.
▶ Shop for correct ingredients.
▶ Prepare food in advance.
▶ Eat regularly.
▶ Drink two litres of water every day.

Department: Relationships
Tasks and objectives:
▶ Arrange and keep to regular dates with my partner.

(Contd)

- ▶ Plan joint activities and quality time together.
- ▶ Speak to parents regularly.
- ▶ Visit parents regularly.
- ▶ Speak to siblings regularly.
- ▶ Visit siblings regularly.
- ▶ Remember all birthdays and anniversaries and send cards/gifts.
- ▶ Schedule calls with friends.
- ▶ Plan lunches with friends.
- ▶ Plan drinks with friends.
- ▶ Plan meals with friends.
- ▶ Plan meetings with colleagues.
- ▶ Plan social events with colleagues.
- ▶ Attend networking events to widen circle of influence.

Now repeat the process, writing out the full job description for each department of your life. You can clearly see everything that you need to keep on top of during the course of each day and week. How do you feel about your life and its structure? Are you on top of everything? Is it all under control? Are you set up in the way that you would like to be?

As you will have observed as you were writing out the details of each area, each one requires a different approach and a different mindset. You will have felt different emotions when writing out the details of your relationships compared to when writing the details of work and career. The feelings you experience when addressing each area will help you determine where to focus your attentions first. If you feel that the structure of a particular area of your life needs to change and will require more than just your efforts to ensure that the progress you desire can take place, now is the time to begin thinking about whom you might need to help you in this area and what form this help will take.

CREATING A NETWORK OF ASSOCIATES, CONTACTS AND RESOURCES

In life it is crucial to have a support network in place. It is vital that jobs get done, and get done effectively. Even the most conservative of life plans can be difficult to achieve single-handed, and for those who wish to strive to reach their full potential, the need for assistance is even greater. For the best possible chance of success, you will need access to a team of experts and specialists to assist you with your objectives. From a reliable plumber to flexible child care and an efficient travel agent, you need people you can rely on to help ease your heavy workload.

Top tip

Start thinking as a manager, not a doer. Just because you are able to do certain tasks doesn't mean you have to do them. Think about the jobs you can delegate, leaving you free to focus on what *really* matters.

Write out the details of specifically who will help you in each area and how they will be of assistance to you. Complete this exercise for each area of your life structure.

Your support network

Department: Health & well-being

Members of support team	How these people help you
Doctor	Appointments and referrals
Dentist	Regular appointments
Gym supervisor	Guidance on exercise programme
Yoga teacher	Teaching sessions
Mother	Look after children while I exercise
Partner	Look after children while I shop
Assistant at work	Schedule my diary to allow shop time

Return to your guiding mantra, 'do it, ditch it or delegate it'. You now have a clearer framework in which to allocate tasks as you can see which department they fit into; you can decide who needs to be responsible for each task and you can direct them on how to perform it. You are now in charge of all operations and for making sure all tasks are completed efficiently. You have responsibility for ensuring that things get done but you don't have to do them all yourself.

Insight

If you have reservations around your ability to manage others, review your list of role models and examine those who are great leaders. Understand what they do to lead well. If you don't have any great leaders on your list of role models, begin researching some straightaway.

Managing and running your life in this way can be a revelation, and the more you can practise planning and strategic management, the easier it will become. Time spent in this area will save you time and energy elsewhere, so make sure you set aside specific slots for planning sessions regularly throughout your day. Formulate a fixed agenda for how your support network is running and how each person is progressing with their tasks. This will make it easier for you to manage and to update progress in all areas and ensure everyone is operating efficiently. Having your network in place and using it efficiently enables you to stay focused on the new and exciting challenges that you set yourself each day.

Effective ways of operating

The secret of getting the best results from yourself and everyone you work with is to be flexible in your approach. What works for you in one area might not be the best approach in another area. And what's effective one day might not be so effective the next day if your mood or the circumstances around you have changed in any way. The key is to know which approach to employ at which time. Here are a few suggestions of approaches that are quick to employ and that work well. You can experiment with them and use them when appropriate.

PRIORITIZING

Look carefully at the jobs on your schedule for the day or the week and give each a score out of ten for how important it is that you get it done. Which jobs are on a deadline and which would you really like to get out of the way? Which tasks have been hanging around for a while and which ones would make you feel fantastic if they were completed? Those tasks with the highest scores are the most urgent.

Visualize yourself having completed these tasks. The very thought of this should make you feel excited and motivated into action. If it doesn't, this may be a sign that some of the tasks aren't really that much of a priority.

For the tasks that are still priorities, score yourself out of ten for how much effort you are prepared to put into each task in order to complete it.

Task	Effort level
1	
2	
3	
4	
5	

Establish what a ten out of ten effort would be and write down what needs to be done.

Task	What must be done for completion
1	
2	
3	
4	
5	

Are you prepared to do everything on this list to complete your tasks?

When you have established what's important, along with how much effort you are willing to give, you are ready to tackle your to-do list and get some results. Begin with the jobs that are most important and for which you are willing to invest the required effort. The results you obtain will be directly related to the effort you put in. Remember, a three out of ten for effort will lead you to a three out of ten result. A ten out of ten score for the effort you are prepared to put in will get a ten out of ten result. Decide what you are prepared to put maximum effort into and then get started on it. Tackling and completing your priority jobs will give you a great sense of satisfaction and make you feel in control of your day.

Top tip

The sooner you can get a positive result each day, the better, but that doesn't mean just tackling the easy stuff first.
Take on the challenges that will bring you the greatest satisfaction on completion and commit to finishing them first.

JOBS TO AVOID

At all costs, avoid starting a number of things that you feel you have a low commitment to completing. You'll only end up with unsatisfactory results or lots of jobs started but not finished.

SINGLE-TASKING

If you have one job that is more important than everything else and that you are fully committed to completing, set aside some time to give it your full attention until it is done. Be realistic with the time you think you need, and pick a time slot when you know you'll be effective. Finish any small, quick tasks that you might find distracting and then mentally prepare yourself for completing the priority task. Make sure your physical environment supports your aims. Place yourself somewhere you won't be disturbed, or explain to others around you that you need some peace and quiet to focus on something important for a while. Make sure you have all the resources you need for the task such as books, research, telephone numbers or contact details, reports or figures. As you reach the time appointed to begin the task, picture yourself carrying it out and finishing it. Imagine how you will feel when it's done. Now you're ready for the job at hand. Get started and enjoy the process of working through to the satisfaction of a job well done. And don't worry about the things you're not doing, you will catch up with your other tasks quickly once you've cleared your head of your most pressing priority.

MULTI-TASKING

If you have a number of jobs that are priorities and that you want to get done in a given time, you need to multi-task. This is an exciting approach to employ and can lead to amazing results.

Your brain does not like things to be left incomplete. This can sometimes be frustrating if you're trying to relax and your unconscious mind keeps reminding you of all the things you have to do. In this situation, remember you have the choice of three different ways of attending to these matters: finish them now, appoint a time to attend to them later, or find another way to get them done – do them, ditch them or delegate them.

The fact that your brain doesn't like to leave issues unsettled can also be used to your advantage. Multi-tasking works by setting your unconscious mind a number of challenges. Because it doesn't like to leave things unfinished, while you focus your mind on getting each job started, your unconscious mind is considering the best ways to complete each one. You can have a number of projects on the go at once and the order in which you return to each job will depend on the solutions that spring to mind once you begin the process.

Multi-tasking

Focus your mind on the number of tasks that you have to do, and the time you are allocating to do them. It might be that you have seven tasks to complete and a whole morning to complete them.

(Contd)

Spend a few minutes thinking about where you want to get to with each task by the end of your allocated time.

Now highlight the first step of the first task and get started on it. When the first step of the first task is complete, quickly move on to the first step of the second task. Get that one started and then move on to the first step of the next task. Continue in this vein until all tasks at hand are underway. Then return to step two of the first task.

Once you are underway, you will find yourself flitting from task to task, perhaps completing more than one step at a time for some tasks or leaving some tasks for a little while before returning to them. This is fine. What really matters is that you end up exactly where you planned to end up with each task at the end of the allotted time.

Multi-tasking is a powerful way of working that some people do more naturally than others. The ability to work like this improves with practice and you will have had experience of operating in this way to one degree or another. Develop this skill and employ it when appropriate.

DEADLINING

This is a similar approach to multi-tasking only you must allocate yourself strict time deadlines for the time you spend on each step of each task. It can be five, ten or fifteen minutes on every step but, whatever chunks of time you decide to operate in, you must stick to this and move on to the next task at the appointed time. Once you've spent the allotted time on each project, you return to the first and spend the same time again on each, in order, until they are all complete.

Deadlining works by focusing your mind on working fast. Often jobs will take up as much time as we give them and sometimes take longer than they really should. Deadlining gives you a limited time for each part of a process, and it is exciting to see what you can come up with in that time.

Top tip

Always monitor what you are doing and how you are doing it. Consider whether you are operating in the most efficient fashion possible or if there is a better way to achieve what you have set out to do.

Whether you are single-tasking, multi-tasking or deadlining, you will be using the combined power of your conscious and unconscious mind to achieve fantastic results.

TIME MANAGEMENT

These are simple examples of ways in which you can manage time. Time is precious so be careful how you spend it and make sure you don't let others rob you of it.

Sticking to your guns when others are demanding your time and attention can be a challenge. If you feel your attention being drawn away from your main priorities, either by others distracting you or you distracting yourself, ask yourself the following questions for every request, challenge or diversion you encounter:

▶ *Does what I am about to attend to fit in with my master plan?*
▶ *What are the benefits of me spending time on this issue?*
▶ *What are the costs of me spending time on this issue?*
▶ *Is this something I really want to spend my time on?*

If the benefits of dealing with a request, an interruption or a diversion outweigh the costs, then the request is worth spending time on. If, after analysing an opportunity, you decide that the costs outweigh the benefits, ignore it and get on with what you were doing.

Gemma is a management consultant with a busy schedule which means that time management is a top priority. Despite being busy, Gemma always made a point of trying to help others but, over time, being helpful had created a situation where Gemma suspected that others weren't respectful of her time and her workload. Because she was always available to assist others, she now felt that they viewed her as someone with plenty of spare time. If they ever needed anything doing, Gemma was always the one they asked. She grew to resent this situation but still found it very awkward to say no when anyone requested anything of her, despite the fact that spending time on other people's work was having a detrimental effect on her own performance.

Gemma began asking herself the questions related to staying focused each time she was interrupted and asked for help. Her answers went as follows:

Does what I am about to attend to fit in with my master plan?

Helping this person out will fit in with my desire to help others, but as far as helping me achieve my overall personal objectives – no – another interruption to help someone will not help me and does not fit in with my master plan.

What are the benefits of me spending time on this issue?

The benefits of helping others are usually the same. I like to be helpful, I like to appear as someone the others can turn to in times of need and I make the effort to help as I hope that they would do the same for me if the roles were reversed.

What are the costs of me spending time on this project?

Each time I say yes to helping someone, I end up behind on what I was doing for myself. It's more than just the time factor now though. I'm beginning to get annoyed with myself for not protecting my space a little more vigorously and I'm annoyed with

CASE STUDY

others for taking my time without seeming to be very appreciative. Having these thoughts continually whizzing through my head is making it even more difficult to focus on my own work. Recently the problem has become unbearable, and by saying yes to so many other people, there just isn't time to do everything and I end up letting down others as well as myself.

Is this something I really want to spend my time on?

Not really, but what else can I do? I don't like saying no when other people ask for help.

Time management and beliefs

Gemma's situation is a common one and highlights decisions that most people go through every day. In isolation, each decision to respond to a request or assist a colleague seems a minor one when, in fact, if you consider all the possible distractions during your day, they can potentially cause a major impact on your ability to perform and achieve what you really want to achieve.

Real life, real people

A question for Gemma was: Why say yes to helping people if it causes such anxiety? As she suggested in the answers to the questions above, she said yes because she didn't like to say no. She didn't like to say no because she held a firm belief that it is important to help people. She had formed this belief when she was young and had held it ever since. It was a belief that had served her well in the past because she found it very satisfying to help others and be appreciated for this, and it was good for her confidence that she was often in possession of knowledge or skills that others didn't have.

In the current situation, Gemma's belief was beginning to have negative consequences for her. She was now concerned that if she said no to too many requests, people would stop asking her for help, which could be a sign that her opinion and her expertise were not valued around the office.

(Contd)

Gemma also believed that it was important to be perceived as knowledgeable, capable, efficient and reliable at work. Saying yes to helping others made Gemma feel that she would be perceived as a valuable member of the team and this would earn her respect. Staying one step ahead with her own workload was also a crucial part of living by this belief.

For a while, her beliefs were aligned and Gemma was perceived in a very positive light in the office. Gradually, her beliefs began to create inner conflict. Too much time helping others meant that Gemma was unable to attend to her own work. Living diligently by one belief was now causing her to compromise in another area, which created a lot of stress. Gemma decided to bring her belief system up to date.

Current beliefs

I believe it is important to help others.

I believe it is important to be perceived as knowledgeable, capable, efficient and reliable at work.

New belief

I believe it is important to help others as long as it doesn't compromise your own position.

Gemma originally set out with a clear belief system and the best of intentions – to be an effective worker and to help others along the way. By focusing wholeheartedly on the good intentions and becoming known as the person to ask for help, she ultimately caused herself a great deal of distress as she compromised her own needs. More than that, by saying yes to every demand that was placed upon her, Gemma gradually ran out of time, both for herself and for others. She continued to say yes to helping out, but then didn't have the time to follow through on this. As a result, Gemma ended up not achieving very much at all and was frustrated by her lack of progress with her own work as well as annoyed with herself when she felt she was letting others down.

Gemma's original belief system created a situation where she set out to be effective and helpful but ended up feeling over-committed and that she was letting everyone down. Her new belief would enable her to attend to her own needs as well as to continue to help others but in a more selective fashion and without cost to herself.

Your time is precious, and you need to be vigilant about where the hours in the day disappear to. Other people can only steal your time if you allow them to. Remember: 'Have your own plan or you'll end up being part of someone else's plan' – this is very true when it comes to time management. If you don't have a strategy for filling your time effectively, others will fill it for you, and probably not with anything that you think is particularly worthwhile or helpful to your objectives.

BE FLEXIBLE

Remember the importance of the flexible approach. On occasions, you will be presented with opportunities that you hadn't anticipated but that will be beneficial to your overall plan for success. It is crucial to keep an open mind when such opportunities arise in order that you don't discount anything that could be useful for you. It's also crucial that a potential opportunity doesn't turn into a hidden distraction. Here are a few questions that will help you to decide between an opportunity and a distraction and to make a judgement on each situation:

▶ **What are my current priorities?**
   What is currently most important to you? Are you spending enough time on these priorities? What else are you currently spending your time on and why?
▶ **Do I have room for another task or project?**
   Once you have established what your priorities are, do you have time to take on anything else and are you willing to rearrange your priorities to accommodate new projects or requests from others?

▶ **Precisely how much work is involved in each request?**
Don't just say yes to someone's request without thinking about exactly what is entailed in the request. It may sound simple enough but the situation could be quite demanding. Agreeing to a simple request to attend a meeting could take up an hour of your time or, if you need to prepare for the meeting, it could take up five hours of your time. Think about the commitment involved before you say yes or no.

▶ **What's in it for me?**
The situation of helping someone else may bring its own opportunities. It's important not to dismiss requests out of hand. There may be some exciting opportunities for you such as learning some new skills or getting exposure to people that can help your career. Always consider the true advantages of helping out – advantages for you as well as for the person requesting the help.

▶ **How much time do I want to spend on this project?**
If you decide you do want to help out, and you've considered how much work could be involved, measure this against how much time you are willing to spend on the project. Think about clever solutions to achieve the advantages of the situation within the time you are willing to allocate.

When you've addressed these issues, you can say yes or no to any request knowing that you are still in charge of your own time and still catering for your own needs.

Insight

Identify your most effective strategy for planning your time. Some people plan an hour or two ahead, others plan one day ahead, some plan weeks at a time. Working with chunks of time that suit you will enable you to balance planning and doing in the right proportion.

SENSE OF PURPOSE

People who fail to take control of their lives often feel as though they are being pulled in many different directions and that their opportunities for progress are limited.

Disjointed life path

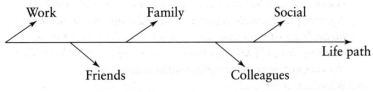

Distractions and limited opportunities

Work Family Social

Life path

Friends Colleagues

External distractions

Those who put themselves in the driving seat feel like they make the decisions on how everything in life moves forward, with a common purpose.

Insight

Imagine if all elements of your life were out of control. You'd struggle to make progress in any area. Now consider a life where every aspect of what you do was under your own control. Tap into the positive feelings you experience with these thoughts and use them to create energy and motivation when faced with challenging situations.

A sense of purpose

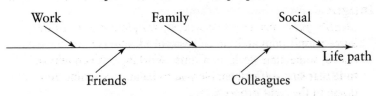

Inspiration and common purpose

Work Family Social

Life path

Friends Colleagues

External motivation and shared goals

When you have achieved the desirable situation of being in full control of your life and your time, you will set about everything you do with a sense of purpose. You will experience renewed vigour and a new-found effectiveness. This purpose will be decided by your mission statement and what's important for you to achieve. With it comes a liberating feeling that you are in charge, making the decisions that matter and pushing life along in the right direction.

> **Top tip**
> Monitor your situation at all times. When new tasks, ideas and projects come on to your radar, quickly assess how important they are and how they fit into your overall plans by giving them a rating out of ten for priority and importance. The things you rate highly are the things you should pay attention to completing. Anything rated low should be discarded or scheduled for attention at some point in the future.

Seven steps to success – getting the most out of everything you do

1 IMMEDIATE ACTION

Think about what you have on your agenda for the rest of today and for tomorrow. Write down a list of all the activities.

2 RING THE CHANGES

Divide your list up into two headings:

Things I want to do   **Things I have to do**

3 PLAN OF ATTACK

Decide on the best way to get all the jobs done and do them well. You may choose to do all the things you want to do and then all the things you have to do, or vice versa. You could set out to alternate between things you have to do and things you want to do.

4 PRIORITIZE

Check out the list of things you have to do and see if you can find a way to turn these tasks into things you want to do, even if it's only that you want to do them so they are complete and off your list.

5 SAY YES

Say yes only to doing everything on your list that is now something that you want to do.

6 SAY NO

Say no to all the tasks that you really couldn't turn into things you wanted to do.

7 DO, DITCH OR DELEGATE

Spend your time doing only those things that you have consciously decided to keep on your list and that you want to do. Delegate anything that needs doing but doesn't make it on to your list of things you want to do. Ditch the rest.

SUMMARY, PRACTICAL ACTIONS AND COMMITMENT

As you perfect the skills to prioritize, to work quickly and to get great results, you will feel a growing sense of control over the way you operate. Over time, you'll feel more comfortable only doing the things that you choose to prioritize and that you want to put maximum effort into. This in turn means that you are constantly occupied by jobs you choose to do and with which you get great results. For everything else on your list, now is the time to use your new-found efficiency and strategic planning skills to ditch them or delegate them.

Chapter 5 is about making the best use of your time so that you get great results from everything you do. Now you know:

▶ *how to structure the business of life*
▶ *the importance of creating your support network*
▶ *approaches that help you function efficiently every day.*

Your commitment is to continually refine your approach so that you are always working to your best advantage and are never sidetracked by interruptions or tasks that are best carried out by others.

New you checklist

At the end of Chapter 5 you will be able to complete the following checklist.

Tick each statement when you are satisfied with your progress in this area:

You know how to prioritize. ☐
You have a support system in place. ☐
You have new approaches to how you work. ☐
You know when and how to say yes, and when
and how to say no. ☐
You live through each day with a sense of purpose. ☐

10 THINGS TO REMEMBER

1 *Choose how to spend your time wisely.*

2 *Tackle tasks quickly, do not procrastinate.*

3 *If you feel procrastination creeping in, research new ways to get things done.*

4 *Dispose of tasks that cause clutter and hamper your progress.*

5 *Delegate wherever possible.*

6 *Promote yourself to leader.*

7 *Practise effective leadership at all times.*

8 *Build a network of contacts and resources to help you out.*

9 *Employ different working strategies to suit your needs at different times.*

10 *Keep an open mind to new ways of working.*

6

Looking great, feeling confident

In this chapter you will learn:
- *how to look your best*
- *how to make a great impression everywhere you go*
- *how to manage your state of mind*
- *how to brim with confidence.*

Changing your perspective on life

Think of a time when you felt great about yourself. Whenever it was in your life, conjure up an image of how you looked, what you were thinking, what others were saying about you and how positive your mindset was. It's a nice feeling, isn't it?

There's no doubt that when you feel positive about yourself, life seems less intimidating, a little more friendly, and somewhat easier to deal with. How effective and how happy do you think you would be if you felt this good all the time?

Insight

Everyone has an area in their life where they feel completely confident. Think about the activities and pastimes in your schedule where you feel great self-confidence and explore what makes you confident in these areas. The ingredients that create confidence in these areas will be transferable to other areas of your life.

As with everything in life, looking and feeling good simply requires a little thought and effort. It's crucial to set aside time to take stock and consider whether or not you are achieving what you want to achieve with your personal appearance and how you dress. The reason why it's so vital is that how you look and what you wear can have such a dramatic influence on your confidence levels, and your confidence levels have such an important bearing on everything you do. You owe it to yourself to make the effort to look great and maximize your confidence levels wherever and whenever you can.

Real life, real people

Here are some examples of what people perceive they would be capable of if they had more confidence:

▶ *Finding a new job.*
▶ *Finding a new partner.*
▶ *Getting a pay rise.*
▶ *Starting their own business.*
▶ *Starting a family.*
▶ *Going to the gym.*
▶ *Socializing more.*
▶ *Standing up for themselves.*
▶ *Being happier.*
▶ *Taking up a new hobby such as singing, dancing or painting.*

CASE STUDY

Confidence levels and looking great

Aim to raise your awareness of the relationship between your appearance and your confidence levels. Analyse how you feel on

different days in a variety of outfits and with different looks.
How do you feel when you dress up? How do you feel when you
dress down? How do you feel when you pick just the right outfit
for an occasion?

PERSONAL APPEARANCE

Your personal appearance includes your haircut, make-up for
women, grooming for men, personal hygiene routine and the
beauty products you use such as perfume or aftershave. What do
all of these things say about you?

HOW YOU DRESS

From top to toe, how you dress will dramatically influence
how you are perceived by others. You'll know when you are
compromising your outfit or cutting corners with a cobbled
together or outdated combination. From now on set a consistently
high standard at all times with what you wear.

UPDATE YOUR LOOK

When was the last time you took a good look at how you present
yourself to the world, and considered how others might view
you? When did you last update your image? Some people convey
a very deliberate image to the world, while others transmit many
messages with their appearance, almost by accident. They don't
think too much about how they look but they're probably the only
ones who don't – you can be sure that everyone else is forming an
opinion on how they look, whether they know it or not and like
it or not. So how can you decide if the image you have now is the
image that works best for you?

Update your look 1

This exercise requires a little time but the results are well worth it. Take a good look in a full-length mirror right now and, starting at the top, look at your hair, face, demeanour, posture, clothes and shoes. Answer the following questions honestly:

▶ What do you think of the person looking back at you?

▶ Is what you see representative of how you feel?

▶ Does what you see represent your personality and your position at home and at work?

▶ Is what you see what you would like others to see?

▶ How confident does this outfit make you feel? Give yourself a score out of ten.

▶ If you were walking down the street and you saw someone matching your reflection, what would you think about that person?

▶ If you were given the opportunity, what comment would you make or what advice would you offer this person on their appearance and presentation?

If you look in the mirror and love what you see, fantastic. Aim to be this happy and this confident with your appearance every single day.

If you look at yourself and you are thinking, 'Well, I wouldn't normally wear this outfit but I was in a bit of a rush this morning' or 'I know my hair needs cutting but I just haven't got around to it', consider the implications of these thoughts. They can be legitimate excuses for not seeing exactly what you might like to see in your reflection, but often it is precisely these thoughts that can nibble away at your confidence and distract you at the most inconvenient moments. Just when you need to be at your most confident, the thought of the suit that you're wearing being a little out of date or your hair looking a bit straggly around the edges can play on your mind and prevent you from giving 100 per cent attention to the situation you are in.

Rightly or wrongly, modern society is a place where people make quick, almost instant, judgements based on appearance. The people you meet will be unaware that every other day of your life you are perfectly turned out in cutting-edge fashion, or that your hair looks sharp and well attended every day apart from today. They will judge what they see right there and then. And, if what they see is combined with you coming across as slightly apologetic because you know you're not looking your best, will you really be making the lasting impression you'd like to make?

Insight

This doesn't mean only impressing others. Choose your outfit based on what will put you in the right frame of mind for whatever you're doing each day. Your outfit will determine your demeanour, your attitudes and your results so select what you wear carefully.

APPEARANCE AND CORE BELIEFS

There is an interesting issue related to this area that sometimes creates conflict, particularly with people who hold a core belief that how you look is not important, it's how you behave and how you perform that really matters. This highlights the area of how much one is willing to compromise on beliefs to achieve a given end. You may believe that what you wear and how you look shouldn't matter, but chances are that you live in an environment where these things are perceived to be important. You must make a decision on whether you need to update this belief if you are looking to achieve the best result in a world where how you look counts for a lot, or whether you leave your belief as it is and accept any limitations that may result from maintaining this belief in a looks-oriented world. Alternatively, you could make sure that you operate only in environments where looks are a low priority. Take a moment now to make sure that your beliefs surrounding your appearance will support you in all your current aims. Do you believe that looks are important? Do you believe in personal grooming or dressing for the occasion? Do you believe it's what's inside that counts?

Insight

It's up to you to choose to update your beliefs or not and a useful rule of thumb is to ask yourself if your current belief is helping you achieve your desired results with your life or obstructing your progress. Answer this question honestly and you can simplify your belief system into one that totally supports your endeavours.

TOTAL CONFIDENCE

Go to your wardrobe and select your favourite outfit. Choose something that you really like and that you know makes you feel good. Take a shower or a bath and get ready as you would if you were going to an important social event or meeting – something you would spend a reasonable amount of time preparing for and something for which you'd really want to look your best. Use your favourite products and put on your chosen outfit.

Now go back to the mirror and revisit the questions.

Answer the following questions honestly:

▶ What do you think of the person looking back at you?

▶ Is what you see representative of how you feel?

▶ Does what you see represent your personality and your position at home and at work?

▶ Is what you see what you would like others to see?

▶ How confident does this outfit make you feel? Give yourself a score out of ten.

▶ If you were walking down the street and you saw someone matching your reflection, what would you think about that person?

▶ If you were given the opportunity, what comment would you make or what advice would you offer them on their appearance and presentation?

How do your answers differ with the change in outfits?

At this point, you should be scoring yourself ten out of ten for how confident you feel in this outfit. If you haven't scored bibliotheca SelfCheck System

Customer Name: MARTIN, MELODY JOY
Customer ID: 1000132804500

Items that you checked out

Title: Be your own life coach
ID: 0000142815562
Due: Friday, August 30, 2019
Messages:
Item checkout ok.

Title: Think and grow rich
ID: 0000144048774
Due: Friday, August 30, 2019
Messages:
Item checkout ok.

Total items: 2
Account balance: $0.00
8/16/2019 11:52 AM
Checked out: 7
Overdue: 0
Hold requests: 0
Ready for pickup: 0
Messages:
Patron status is ok.

Thank you for using the bibliotheca SelfCheck
System.

a ten yet, be honest about what is missing from the finished picture. It might be that you want to change your hairstyle, shoes, tie, some aspect of your grooming, but whatever it is you must choose a time when you will fix it. Book your haircut or set aside some time to get to the shops to buy what you need to complete your image. When you have what you require for your perfect look and outfit, return to the mirror and focus on the ten out of ten presentation of yourself.

Top tips

▶ Always consider your outfits well in advance. Last-minute panic over what to wear rarely leads to good choices.

▶ Have a few reliable back-up outfits that you are comfortable wearing. If you can't find the right thing on any given day, at least you have these outfits as a fallback option rather than choosing something you know doesn't really work.

▶ If something you wear makes you uncomfortable, get rid of it at the end of the day. Keeping clothing that doesn't work for you will only cost you time in the future as you wonder all over again, should you wear it, what does it go with, and so on. You already know it doesn't work for you so get it out of your wardrobe and out of your mind.

Hold on to the positive feelings

As you look at your ten out of ten reflection, you will feel confident and powerful. Wouldn't it be great to feel this way all the time?

There is a technique in coaching that enables you to do just that. It's called 'anchoring' and it is a very simple way of instantly achieving your most positive state of mind. Using the technique enables you to perform at your best and most effective whenever you need to and whatever the circumstances. Anchoring provides easy access to your most optimistic outlook on the world, ready for use whenever you need it. Now wouldn't that be handy?

HOW DOES IT WORK?

The human brain cannot distinguish between a real event and an imagined event. You will experience this if you think about something in your life, perhaps something happy or sad, with such intensity that you can create all the emotions of the event as if it were actually happening. You may be happily going about your daily business when a sad thought will pop into your head. If you focus on this thought and let it grow you can feel genuinely sad although nothing has actually changed with your life at that moment. All that has changed is your mood.

Similarly, you may be struggling with a difficult project, feeling busy, tired and fed up. Suddenly, you remember that you're going to visit your favourite friends at the weekend. You haven't seen them for ages and you're really excited about the trip. The more you think about how good it's going to be, the more your mood is elevated. You're still in the middle of your project but you now feel a whole lot better. You can take a breath, sit up straight and get on with what you're doing with renewed vigour.

In these situations, a simple reaction occurs, beginning with a thought that creates emotion which leads to a physical response. If you're elbow-deep in paperwork, chances are you may be experiencing low energy, your body might feel heavy and your brain a little bit sluggish. Then you remember your fun weekend ahead and you immediately feel the emotions that go with that thought. Your mood is lifted and your body language changes to reflect your change in mood.

The purpose of anchoring is to use the close association between the mental process and the physical reaction to control the way you perform in various situations. Rather than wait for positive thoughts to come to you, you can reverse the process and generate a positive thought when you need it by creating a physical trigger.

ANCHORING MADE SIMPLE

As you go about your daily routine you will already use examples of anchoring. Anchoring processes are like rituals and routines that put us into specific states for particular purposes. In the morning you may get ready in a particular order to best prepare yourself for the day. At work, you may need to tidy your desk and get a coffee before you get stuck into the business of the day.

The purpose of these rituals is to associate positive thoughts with the physical behaviours. The routines act like triggers to a particular mindset and you know that if you act in a certain way, you will feel a certain way.

HOW TO CREATE YOUR POSITIVE ANCHOR

First you need to find a physical gesture with which to associate and anchor your positive feelings. It needs to be something that you don't often do, so choose carefully or you run the risk of firing your anchor when it's not needed. It also needs to be something that won't be noticeable to others. Squeezing your thumb and the tip of your third finger together is a good example. If you happen to do this as a regular habit, then choose something different.

Take a good look at your ten out of ten reflection and focus on the positive feelings that run through your body and mind. Concentrate on where the feelings are located in your body and your mind. Imagine those feelings growing to gradually inhabit the whole of your being until you are radiating positivity.

Close your eyes and think of a time when you were feeling totally confident in your own abilities. You may have just performed well in a meeting or had some positive feedback. You feel as though you could take on any challenge. Focus entirely on that feeling and where it is in your body. Feel it grow and at the same time touch your third finger and thumb together.

Relax your hand and think of a time when you were feeling totally happy and satisfied with the world. You may have just had a great day, or you might be contemplating a great day to come, but choose a time when you were totally in the moment, caught up in what you were doing and feeling as happy as you ever have in your life. Concentrate on what that feels like, where you were, what you were doing, what you could see, the sounds you could hear. Focus on making everything clearer, brighter, stronger until you feel that happiness overwhelm you and then touch your third finger and thumb together as the emotions peak.

Relax your hand and think of a time when you felt powerful – a time when you were in control of your situation and totally at ease with everything around you. Picture how great it feels to step back to that time. Imagine the details of how the scene around you, the chatter in the background and the noises in your head, all seemed to be focused in one direction and that direction was your success, your drive, your ability, your power at that particular time. As you relive the time when you were totally in charge and completely absorbed in the moment, touch your third finger and thumb together.

Relax your hand, take a deep breath and open your eyes. You now have a positive anchor ready and waiting to be fired. Take a look at your reflection again. With all these positive thoughts and emotions running through your mind, you now feel ready for anything.

FIRING YOUR POSITIVE ANCHOR

Now that you've associated such positive feelings so closely with a physical gesture, you are able to run the process in reverse. By touching your third finger and thumb together and firing your anchor at any time of the day, you will instantly feel these positive emotions flooding through you. Your posture and body language will alter, your mental state will change and you will feel confident, happy and powerful, immediately.

GROWING YOUR POSITIVE ANCHOR

Now that you have a positive anchor, you can add or stack as many different positive emotions and feelings in the same place as you like. Stack actual events on to your anchor as they happen. Whenever you have a success or triumph or you catch yourself caught in a moment where you feel happy, content, relaxed, confident or satisfied, touch your third finger and thumb together and anchor this moment and these feelings for use in the future.

Cultivate the right attitude

Cheerfulness and contentment are great beautifiers and are famous preservers of youthful looks.

Charles Dickens

You will now be able to fire your positive anchor whenever you want to brim over with confidence. Feeling confident in situations will allow you to perform to the best of your abilities, which will enhance your performance and in turn lead to growing confidence. Looking great and feeling confident are powerful character traits, and you will notice how the reaction of others towards you alters as you become more comfortable living with these traits as part of your character and attitude. Think about the people you know who look great and appear confident. Consider the reactions they experience as they go about their daily business and use this information to refine your sense of what it is to look great and make the impression you want to make wherever you go.

Insight

Feeling confident is a skill to be practised as regularly as possible. You can enhance the process by clearly visualizing events before they take place. The more confident you are in your visualization, the more confident you will be when the event takes place.

Seven steps to success – looking great, feeling confident

1 IMMEDIATE ACTION

Stop right now and consider what you're wearing and how you look. Is it representative of who you are and who you want to be? Write down what's working and what's not.

2 RING THE CHANGES

This bit is fun. Set aside some time to clear out your bedroom, wardrobes, cupboards, drawers and your bathroom of all clothes and grooming products that you don't use and don't need. Take what's worth taking to the charity shop and throw away the rest. If the thought of this scares you and you think you might need some of the items, put everything into black bags and leave them in a corner of the spare room or the garage. If you haven't looked into the bags by the time a month has passed, you're definitely safe to get rid of them.

3 PLAN OF ATTACK

Look at what's left in your wardrobe and what beauty or grooming products you now have and decide on anything new you might need so that you can present the image you want at all times. Be disciplined so that you're not just buying another load of clutter, but have some fun and buy things you really want and that will really make a difference.

4 PRIORITIZE

Pick something out that is representative of you as a happy and confident character and wear it soon. The quicker you get into the new you, the better.

5 REVIEW

Be vigilant at all times. The new you will continue evolving so make sure you keep up to date with wearing only things that work for you.

6 PACK UP THE POSITIVES

Take note of each moment when you feel happy, confident, positive and optimistic. Analyse why you feel like that at any given moment. Store these moments for use in the future.

7 CONTROL YOURSELF

Fire your positive anchor whenever you need a boost.

SUMMARY, PRACTICAL ACTIONS AND COMMITMENT

At all times, you are in control of the image you present to the world and how you look and how you feel in any situation. Choose your look and your wardrobe carefully, based on what makes you feel great. Visualize your day ahead and know what outfit and approach will work best for you. Consider your role models and what they would wear in your situation and how they would approach the day. Fire your positive anchor when you need a quick boost. Acknowledge your positive moods and successes during each day and add them to your anchor.

> Chapter 6 is about raising your awareness of the image you portray. Now you know:
>
> ▶ *that how you look and feel is up to you*
> ▶ *how to dress for success*
> ▶ *how to create and maintain a positive mindset.*

Your commitment is to always put yourself at the best advantage. Dress appropriately for all occasions in outfits that make you feel on top of the world and create the most positive mindset for every situation you enter into.

New you checklist

At the end of Chapter 6 you will be able to complete the following checklist.

Tick each statement when you are satisfied with your progress in this area:

You are happy with how you present yourself. ☐
You feel confident with your image. ☐
You have a positive anchor. ☐
You can create your most positive mindset when you need it. ☐

10 THINGS TO REMEMBER

1 *Confidence breeds success.*

2 *Being confident is a skill that can be practised and perfected.*

3 *Acknowledge when you are confident and develop confidence skills into other areas.*

4 *Dress for success at all times.*

5 *Decide the messages you wish to send with your appearance and present yourself accordingly.*

6 *Ensure your beliefs around personal appearance are consistent with your life objectives.*

7 *Anchor all positive experiences.*

8 *Choose your public persona and attitudes and practise them in private.*

9 *Review your personal appearance regularly to remain contemporary.*

10 *Reinvent yourself when appropriate.*

Beautiful body, endless energy

In this chapter you will learn:
- *how to make exercise a part of your daily routine*
- *strategies for healthy eating*
- *how to guarantee the energy and the body shape you've always wanted.*

Shaping up for success

As you know from the previous chapter, if you look great, you will feel great. Looking great comes both from your outer appearance and from within – your inner glow. In this chapter you will discover the secrets to great health, fantastic fitness, optimum energy and the body shape you desire.

Many people spend much of their time and energy experimenting with quick-fix fitness plans or the latest diets and food regimes. This chapter will show you once and for all how to find a routine with your fitness and your food that really works for you and gives you the results you've always wanted and the body and the energy you need for life.

Good health

Thankfully, the majority of people in the Western world benefit from relatively good health and are not suffering from or limited by any major disease or illness. Usually, perceptions of health revolve around how you feel on a day-to-day basis. Generally, provided you are able to do everything you need to do, you are happy enough and prepared to put up with the stresses and strains of modern life. You keep busy each day working, looking after others, grabbing some food when you can, taking care of chores and 'the stuff of life', socializing, and looking after yourself if you can fit it in. Hopefully you arrive at the end of the day with a little bit of time to unwind and relax before getting off to bed to rest before starting the routine all over again the next day.

In these circumstances, the fact that there are opportunities to live another way is often overlooked. These days, taking care of oneself is sometimes seen as an added extra in life – something that you can do if you have time, but really there are other more important things to be getting on with.

Now is the time to look at this notion from a different perspective – a perspective that puts your health and well-being at the top of the list of priorities rather than at the bottom. After all, without your health, nothing else in life will be possible, and certainly much of what you do will be made more difficult.

Taking the time to look after yourself properly will ensure that you are capable of fulfilling all of your dreams. What's also important to remember is that good health will enable you to get more out of everything you do. There is currently a lot of importance attached to what you do. Days are busy and to-do lists are endless and the most important thing is that you get through it all. But what about your enjoyment and fun factor during each of your busy days?

Taking care of yourself gives you energy, confidence and a positive outlook. You are better able to deal with the challenges of life and in a far better position to enjoy the things you do. Take this opportunity to say goodbye to thinking of healthy living as being in conflict with your current life and as something that will get in the way of your effectiveness, that is, just another thing to add to the list. Instead, see it as something in harmony with the rest of life, a way of nourishing yourself to be better at everything you do, a means of being able to put more into life and of getting more out of it – to be happier and more fulfilled on a daily basis.

Insight

Resolve now to look forward to every day as an opportunity to make the most out of your life and make progress with your personal development. Too many people approach each day expecting it to be difficult and tiring and that it will take some toll on their personal well-being. Choose instead to nourish and develop your mind and body daily and you'll approach everything you do with renewed energy and motivation.

In a world obsessed by physical appearance, not a day will go by without a newspaper, magazine or television programme advising you on what to eat or how to be more active. If you tried to pay attention to all the advice, you'd suffer information overload. You must be selective with what you take on board and implement into your life. The most straightforward way to make successful changes is to consider how what you read or see on television relates to your situation. Why and how does healthy living matter to you? Thinking about the personal applications of being healthier will be the key to your success.

Why do I want to live a healthier life?

Write down all the ways in which living a healthier life will benefit you. List everything you can come up with. Your answers will probably include some of the topics we've touched on already in the book. Make sure you include all the reasons that are personal to you.

Living a healthier life will enable me to:

▶ live longer
▶ live more happily
▶ have better energy
▶ be more comfortable with myself
▶ be more focused
▶ experience greater self-esteem
▶ be able to fit into nicer clothes
▶ be more confident.

Keep going until you have as many reasons as possible for making changes in this area. Put this list in order of importance to you and then keep it handy. It will drive you on if ever you feel your motivation waning. If you're thinking about skipping your exercise class, this list will remind you why it's worth going. If you're tempted by something you know you'd really rather not be eating, this list shows you why you want to make the right choices.

Healthy living and coaching

Some people love being healthy, others hate it. So what makes the difference between the two viewpoints? And how can everyone come to enjoy exercise and healthy food?

Clearly there is more to healthy living than just taking exercise and eating well. Living a healthier life can change your perspective forever and, because the results of the exercise you do and the food you eat have such a crucial bearing on how you look and how you feel, it's not an area you can afford to ignore or take lightly. This is why healthy living is so important to many people, and this is also why it is a useful process to work with your health and fitness objectives to practise the techniques you've been learning in this book. For further details on the specifics of effective exercise and nutrition plans, read *Teach Yourself Fitness*.

Healthy living and exercise

Top tips
The golden rules of successful exercise

Experiment with different approaches until you find an exercise routine that works for you. Your routine could consist of walking, running, swimming, cycling, a gym routine, a combination of gym classes, horse riding, sailing, netball, football, rugby or dancing. It doesn't matter what exercise you like doing, what matters is that you do it. And you are far more likely to do it, and do it regularly, if you enjoy it.

Establish a balance with exercise that works for you. Magazines will tell you that you shouldn't exercise too late in the day or that it is only worth exercising if you can do it at six o'clock in the morning before breakfast. Some believe you need to exercise every day for 15 minutes, others will tell you that three times a week for 90 minutes is more successful. The government recommends exercising for 30 minutes, five days a week. But how does exercise fit into your life? You need to find the schedule that works for you, both now and for the long term. Far better to exercise twice a week at times that suit you forever, than to aim to exercise first thing every day and then run out of steam after a couple of weeks or, worse still, never even get started.

Find good reasons to make exercise work for you and focus on these at all times. Occasionally, the idea of taking exercise will not fill you with joy. At these times, concentrating on all the positives that come with exercise will spur you into action and enable you to push through these moments. You will undoubtedly feel better after taking some exercise and it is these feelings you should focus on if you find yourself wavering. Focus on the satisfaction of completing your exercise, rather than the process of exercising. The most common reason why people achieve limited success with making changes in this area is that they focus their attention on the discomfort and inconvenience involved in making the changes. They think too much about the effort involved in getting to the gym or going out for a run. They contemplate changing the way they eat but quickly become overwhelmed by the thought of having to shop differently and think of new ideas for meals and snacks, or they become hung up on what they might miss out on. Success with making changes to your health comes with bypassing these thoughts and skipping straight to the reasons why it will be worth the effort. Focus directly on what's in it for you and the actions that will lead you to these results will become much easier to implement.

EXERCISE AND PRIORITIZING

Rate your satisfaction with how healthy your life is at the moment and decide how important it is that you do something to change the situation. Living a healthier life has to be a high priority for you in order to create the motivation to make the necessary changes.

EXERCISE AND GOAL-SETTING/PLANNING

You must be clear and explicit about where you are now with your fitness in contrast to where you would like to be. Establish what changes in your approach and your behaviour would bridge the gap between where you are now and where you want to be. Outline an initial approach for making these changes and build some flexibility into your plan. Set specific times to get going and outline clear milestones along the way when you can assess your progress so far against your desired progress, and you can update your approach as necessary.

EXERCISE AND BELIEFS

Think carefully about why you want to make changes with your health and fitness and what making these changes will actually give you. How will your life be better? You must be absolutely clear on how you will benefit from your new exercise routine or you may struggle to put it into action. Update your beliefs to ensure they are in line with what you want to achieve. Holding beliefs such as 'I'm fat', 'I'm lazy' or 'I just don't like exercise' will slow your progress. New beliefs such as 'I'm on the way to my new body', 'Exercising helps me feel energized' or 'Exercise is an important part of my life' will increase your chances of success.

EXERCISE AND VISUALIZATION

Ultimately, you must believe that you will succeed with your objectives and you must plan and visualize every step of the way. Take the time to picture what the new you will look like. Imagine what you will wear, how you will feel, what you will think about your own success, what others will say about your achievements. Believe it, visualize it and commit to it 100 per cent. Picture yourself exercising and enjoying it. Anticipate how you will feel following each workout. Imagine telling others how good you feel about reaching your goals.

EXERCISE AND MODELLING

Recall examples of times in your life when you were active and felt good being so. It doesn't matter how far back you need to go, what matters is that you remember positive associations with exercise or activity. Everyone has at least one positive experience, whether it be cycling around in the summer holidays or swimming in the ocean on holiday. Remember how good this felt and then aim to recreate these feelings with the exercise in your current routine.

Select some positive role models for your health and fitness. Who do you know who looks like you want to look? Who has that inner glow and positive demeanour that comes with regular activity? Quiz these people and find out how they do it. Model the aspects of their approach that are applicable to your particular situation.

EXERCISE AND ANCHORING

When you commit totally to your objective, ensure that all your behaviour supports you. Anchor your positive feelings during and after each workout and fire your anchor if you ever feel your motivation wane.

Insight

Getting active is something that many people struggle to fit into their routine, yet when they master it their lives are enhanced in many ways. Take this opportunity to revisit previous chapters of this book and apply as many techniques as possible to shaking up your activity routine to ensure you achieve the results you deserve.

Healthy living and nutrition

Top tips
The golden rules of successful healthy eating

Do not aim for 100 per cent textbook perfection. Instead, decide what the perfect eating plan would look like for you. Choose a balance that suits you, such as eating healthily 80 per cent of the time and not worrying about what you eat for 20 per cent of the time. Be honest about where the balance currently lies for you – you might currently eat well for 50 per cent of the time and not for 50 per cent of the time –

(Contd)

and set a deadline for when you want to have reached your chosen balance.

Implement change gradually. For one week, keep a record of all that you eat and drink, and the times that you consume these products. This diary provides written evidence of the food plan that gives you the results you are living right now. Writing everything down will show you where you can quickly make changes. Decide on one or two changes to aim for each week until you have made these changes your new habits. Keep each week's diary so you can track your changes, and eventually you will have a written record of the weekly routine that results in the body shape and energy levels that you desire.

Plan ahead. Healthy eating begins with looking at your schedule. Examine where you will be and what you will be doing over the coming days. Establish what you will be eating during these days. The biggest threat to eating healthily is not having accessibility to good food choices, so plan your meals and snacks around your schedule and make sure you're never far away from food that you know works for you. Keep your fridge stocked with ingredients for staple meals, quick meals and snacks. If you foresee particularly busy days ahead or days when you are on the move a lot, prepare food in advance, both for eating at home and for eating when you are out and about. Shopping for the right food products is an integral part of your healthy eating routine.

Keep your metabolism firing on all cylinders. Skipping meals will slow your metabolism, leaving you feeling sluggish and clinging on to extra calories you don't need. Eating regularly will keep your metabolism running fast and burning calories at all times. The golden rules here are never to go more than four hours without food and never eat more food at a single sitting than you can fit in two cupped hands. For some people, observing these rules may mean they don't need to adjust the total amount of food they eat but simply need to make sure the food is of good quality and is spaced out more evenly throughout the day.

NUTRITION AND PRIORITIZING

Rate your satisfaction with how healthy your food routine is at the moment and decide how important it is that you do something to change the situation. Refer back to your reasons why living a healthier life is important for you now, and make sure that eating healthily is a top priority for you before you attempt any lasting changes.

NUTRITION AND GOAL-SETTING/PLANNING

Be specific about the changes you are setting out to make with your eating plan. Keep your objectives simple, such as 'By the end of the month I will eat breakfast every day', 'I will eat four pieces of fruit every day from now on, two mid-morning and two mid-afternoon'. Plan how you will support yourself in your objectives. If you want to eat breakfast every day, you need to shop for some breakfast options and have them in stock. If you want to eat more fruit, you will need to create a new routine of shopping regularly for fresh supplies so that you have plenty at home or at work when you need it. Review your objectives regularly so that you can quickly address and adjust your behaviour if necessary.

NUTRITION AND BELIEFS

Investigate whether your beliefs around healthy eating will help or hinder you in your new objective. Beliefs such as 'Food just isn't a priority for me' or 'I've always been overweight' will limit your success. New beliefs along the lines of 'I'm interested in food as a means to reach my desired body shape' or 'I decide what weight I'd like to be and am in control of this' will help you achieve great results quickly.

NUTRITION AND VISUALIZATION

From the beginning of your healthy eating regime, you must create mental images of yourself shopping for healthy food, preparing interesting meals packed with energy and vitamins and nutrients, eating them and, above all, enjoying them.

The more pictures you can create in your mind of the benefits you will gain from healthy eating, such as a new body shape, fat loss, new clothes and how you will feel shopping for them and wearing them, increased energy, better skin and a radiant glow from within, the easier it will be to make the necessary behaviour changes and the quicker you will begin living these positive images.

NUTRITION AND MODELLING

Remember times in your life when you ate well and how you felt about this. Recall as many positive, personal associations with healthy eating as you can. These recollections could be times when you have made an effort to cook for yourself, healthy and enjoyable meals you have eaten in restaurants or times when someone else has cooked for you.

Who do you know that eats well and lives with the benefits of doing so? Select a few people who have a successful approach to healthy eating and find out how they do it. Quiz them on what they find easy or where the pitfalls are. Learn from their experience and tailor an approach that suits you.

NUTRITION AND ANCHORING

Every time you eat well or shop for good food and feel positive for doing so, create an anchor in order that you can access these positive feelings whenever you need them. Stack more positive feelings on the same anchor when you lose weight, change shape and buy and wear new clothes. There may be difficult spots along the way, but firing your anchor and experiencing all your great feelings that go with eating well and achieving your goals will easily see you through these challenges.

Insight

Eating well to achieve great energy and effective weight management can be a challenge within a busy schedule. Almost everyone has changes they'd like to make in this area so it's a further effective working example to put the skills you've learned so far into action. Review what you've read so far in this book and begin applying the key techniques to making progress with your food routine immediately. Start with a small change and build from there.

Real life, real people

CASE STUDY

Heather wanted to live a healthier life, begin exercising and alter her approach to food so she sought coaching to help her get started. She had exercised sporadically in the past and knew from experience that her ability to exercise was more in her head than her body. When she managed it she felt pretty fit and was glad to be doing something active. She had also had periods of eating well but these tended to be short-lived. What she really wanted was to work on her mental approach so that she could establish strategies that would enable her to make exercise and eating well part of her long-term future.

Heather's desire to live more healthily is a common one and, on the face of it, a seemingly easy objective to achieve. As it turned out, Heather's situation proved to be a great example of how, in order to achieve a seemingly simple objective, one may have to tackle a number of more complex issues along the way. It was clear from the outset that Heather's objectives were about more than simply feeling a little healthier.

Prioritizing

Heather's husband had died a year previously. Heather had to cope with his long illness before he died, deal with the grief and the loss when he died, and at the same time look after their young son. Although this was a painful process, it enabled Heather to formulate some really good reasons why she wanted to make specific changes to her life now and become more active.

1 Heather's husband died from cancer at a young age. Although she knew she couldn't achieve full control over this area in as much as she could never guarantee she wouldn't become ill,

(Contd)

Heather knew that she could take steps to put herself in the best possible condition for staying healthy. This is what she resolved to do, both for herself and for her son.

2 Heather knew, deep down, that getting more active would make her feel more optimistic about life in general. Even with her own limited experience of this, she knew enough to appreciate that exercising and eating healthily would go some way to creating positive energy and a better frame of mind.

3 Heather knew that at some point, maybe not just yet, she would want to return to the dating scene and so she wanted to take some steps to work on how she looked and how she felt about herself in preparation for this time.

Immediately there were positive incentives for Heather to make healthy choices in life and to make them sooner rather than later. Dealing with the situation with her husband had been Heather's priority for a long time. She was now ready to make herself a priority.

Goal-setting/planning

Heather decided what kind of exercise she was prepared to do, which was a combination of running, skipping, strength training and stretching. She would also swim and cycle with her son at the weekends. She decided what changes she would make to her diet, which included adding a fruit smoothie for breakfast, eating salads and sushi for lunch rather than always having sandwiches, and making sure that she ate enough each day to keep her metabolism running fast and burning calories. She set herself a target weight, and identified which of her clothes that were currently a little tight she wanted to get into within six weeks and which within twelve weeks.

Beliefs

Heather believed that life would be better if she could get active, improve her energy levels and change her body shape.

She also held a couple of limiting beliefs. First, her husband had been fit and yet had still become ill. This led Heather to believe that exercise might not have any bearing on health. She also had strong negative associations with healthy eating. Her husband had required an incredibly healthy diet when he was ill but the act of preparing healthy meals now reminded Heather very strongly of that period, which was obviously distressing. It was vital for Heather at this stage to update her belief system to take account of her objectives, aside from the situation with her husband, and ensure that she could focus on her goals without any distractions. She selected two new beliefs:

1 Exercise may not prevent illness but living a healthy life is more fulfilling than living an unhealthy life.
2 Healthy eating has more relevance to the future with her son than the past with her husband.

Visualization

Heather created images in her mind of herself running in the park, exercising at home, and cycling and swimming and having fun with her son. She also worked on creating images of herself preparing healthy meals and feeling good about doing it. Finally, she booked some future social engagements and then began thinking about how she would look and feel when these engagements came around in light of the positive changes she was making.

Modelling

Heather had exercised in the past so she had positive experiences to recall and focus on. She also had two role models, one a friend and one a work colleague, both of whom took regular exercise, ate well, had great energy and appeared to experience a lot of fun in their lives. Heather resolved to set aside some time to find out a little more about how they managed it.

(Contd)

Anchoring

Heather began her new routine with gusto and made good progress. Something she discovered along the way was that, while she enjoyed her exercise, sometimes she found it much easier than at other times. This resulted in progress being a little slower than it could have been.

Heather recognized that she had to capture the positive feelings and emotions that she felt during some of her workouts and recall these feelings when she wasn't feeling quite so motivated. For a number of sessions, she took a few moments at the end to acknowledge just how positive she was feeling and how those feelings had come about through the activities she had successfully achieved. Gradually, Heather created a positive anchor associated with feeling great following exercise. Then, instead of focusing on when she was going to exercise next, she simply concentrated on when she wanted to feel these feelings again. Whenever she thought about exercise and felt less than 100 per cent motivated, Heather simply fired her anchor, experienced the positive emotions and removed any hesitation about getting active again.

Success

Clearly, Heather's situation was more complicated than just living a little more healthily. She had to do some groundwork in order to create the correct circumstances for success and, by taking the time to do this, she increased her chances of reaching her goal and reaching it quickly. Follow the same procedure and you too will experience fantastic results.

Insight

Remember that success with your fitness routine and your eating pattern take a little bit of time and effort, but when you have the actions and behaviours in place that ensure you achieve your goals in these areas, you don't need to think much about exercise or food at all, you simply follow the routines that you know work for you.

Seven steps to success – beautiful body, endless energy

1 IMMEDIATE ACTION

Get into the mindset of someone who lives a fantastically healthy lifestyle. Get yourself a glass of water and then prepare a fruit smoothie or some freshly squeezed juice. Check your posture, sit up straight and have a bit of a stretch. Think about how your body feels.

2 RING THE CHANGES

Your body and mind from now on are going to feel different. Make a list of everything that you want to eliminate or cut down on. Things like processed food, caffeine, alcohol, crisps or sweet snacks. Check the list and make sure that you are happy to live with less of these things in your life. For those you can't completely get rid of, decide what will be an acceptable level for them to feature in your new routine.

3 PLAN OF ATTACK

Devise your healthy living routine for the next seven to ten days. Consider what you want to eat and drink for these days. Plan when you will exercise and what you will do.

4 PRIORITIZE

Select which measures for healthy living you can put into place the fastest. The sooner you start, the quicker you will feel great.

5 REVIEW

Healthy living is addictive, so keep track of the changes you make so that you can make more of them. You don't know how fantastic you could feel until you put as many positive strategies into place as possible.

6 MAKE IT FUN

Get others involved where you can. If you are living healthily with other people, not only will you be more likely to stick to your objectives but it will be more fun to share the experience and success with others.

7 ENJOY IT

From the moment you begin to live a healthier life, you will feel better, so start enjoying it right away. Don't wait until you achieve one of your milestones to celebrate your success. You can revel in these triumphs when they come as well, but for now take heart and motivation from the fact that you have begun the journey.

SUMMARY, PRACTICAL ACTIONS AND COMMITMENT

Success with healthy living objectives is within your control. You must be vigilant at all times and regularly assess where you are in relation to where you want to be with your exercise and your food routine. Update your approach regularly to continue making positive steps.

Chapter 7 is about achieving the health and the body you desire. Now you know:

▶ *how to question yourself at a deeper level with regard to healthy living*
▶ *how to apply coaching strategies to healthy living*
▶ *how to guarantee results.*

Your commitment is to continue evolving your approach until you have a variety of strategies that will get you whatever results you are looking for. Make a note of which measures lead to each specific result so that if you want to tone up, you know what to do. If you want to maintain your current physique, you know which plan to follow. If you want more energy, you have a strategy that will get you more energy. Refine these strategies and use them whenever you need them. And don't just think about using them, get them into action as soon as you can.

New you checklist

At the end of Chapter 7 you will be able to complete the following checklist.

Tick each statement when you are satisfied with your progress in this area:

You have a fitness routine that works.	☐
You have an eating plan that works.	☐
You see results.	☐
You feel results.	☐

10 THINGS TO REMEMBER

1 *Every fitness or food plan in the world will have limitations when applied to your situation.*

2 *Only a well researched plan that fits into your lifestyle will give you the results you deserve.*

3 *Healthy living is a key foundation to success in all areas of your life.*

4 *Focus on why healthy living matters to you.*

5 *Be flexible with your approach and be prepared to try new activities and foods.*

6 *Create healthy living plans that work for all your circumstances – home, work, holidays, travel, weekdays and weekends.*

7 *Take charge of your situation and work on it alone or seek the help and support of others. Decide which strategy will work best for you.*

8 *Explore why you may not have achieved your desired results in this area in the past and make sure any lurking barriers to current success are addressed and removed.*

9 *Take action that supports your health every single day.*

10 *Challenge any excuses you feel creeping into your mind and refocus on your end goal.*

8

Shape up your finances

In this chapter you will learn:
- *to appreciate your earning power and earn what you are worth*
- *where you can make savings*
- *how to create financial security*
- *to adopt a positive attitude to money*
- *to generate wealth and prosperity.*

Achieving the correct mindset for money

Do you have enough money? Do you know how much would be enough for you?

Like most people, you probably think that you would like more money, and it's probably true that a little extra income would ease the pressures of life and give you a few more options on how you spend your time, but how much money would you really like to have? How much do you realistically need? How much do you want?

This chapter will help you to work out how much you'd like to have, how you can get it, and what you'll do with it when you have it. There are suggestions for new ways of approaching your financial situation, some simple strategies to save money and make the most of what you have, and suggestions on how to alter your mindset to end money worries for good.

In 2005, Rebecca sought coaching to help her improve her financial situation. She had a job that she really enjoyed and which paid well, but she was also the main earner in her family and, following a period without a pay rise and with two growing children and a dog to look after, she felt it was the right time for a salary rise.

The first thing Rebecca needed to establish was what she thought she was worth to her employer and why. Once she had answered some key questions on the specific details of how much her salary should be and how she could earn and justify every part of this – see below – she was able to confidently negotiate a new deal for herself, and surprised even herself with the great result she achieved of a salary rise of 25 per cent.

When we do more than we are paid to do, eventually we will be paid more for what we do.
Zig Ziglar, American sales trainer and motivational author and speaker

Rebecca's situation demonstrates very clearly the importance of quickly bridging the gap between highlighting a desire in oneself that something needs to change, and taking steps to make it happen. She knew she deserved a pay rise; she simply had to establish and carry out the steps to lead her towards her aim. In order for you to achieve similar results, to earn what you want to earn and, just as importantly, what you are worth, you first need to be clear in your own mind on what these figures are. Answer the following questions in as much detail as you can.

Earn what you're worth

▶ Write down how much you currently earn.

▶ How much money do you think your intellect, ideas and contribution are worth to your employer or to your business? Think carefully because what you think you are worth is what you will earn. Be honest about your value, know that you deserve it so you can justify it and negotiate for it.

▶ What do you do in your current role or business that generates the most value? If you were to do this aspect of your job only, then what would you be worth? Answering this question will help you to calculate your maximum value to your employer or business. It also highlights what you should be spending your time working on. All other tasks should be managed or delegated.

▶ What is your Unique Selling Point (USP) to your business? What do you do that no one else can? How unique is your USP to your business? What can you do to stand out even more? How valuable does that make you as an asset?

▶ Based on your answers to the above questions, write down how much you should be earning.

▶ Formulate a plan for when you will be earning this amount. Who will you be working for and what will you be doing? What steps do you need to take to ensure you negotiate yourself into this position?

▶ Ensure your plan contains information on how you will spend your increased earnings when you reach your objective. After all, there's no point having it if you're not going to do something useful with it, is there? What will you do with your extra income?

(Contd)

> ► What is the first action that you can take today to put
> your plan into action and begin heading towards your
> desired earnings?

Finance and values

The desire to earn more money was prompted in Rebecca by one
of her core values – security for herself and her family. The need
to uphold this value enabled her to make some changes and really
improve her life. Security is a basic need for most people, but what
happens when it has been obtained? Should you stop there and be
happy with your lot? You may have become conditioned to push
things on to the next level and achieve the best for yourself and those
around you. But what are you actually trying to achieve at this point?

Insight
Your financial situation provides a good example of a more
general coaching approach which is that you must review
regularly to ensure that you are where you want to be. As
life moves on, your financial commitments will change and
you must make sure that you are always one step ahead
by assessing your current financial situation against what's
coming next in your life.

Real life, real people

Angela was desperate to be promoted at work. She felt strongly
that the extra money that would come with a promotion would
improve her life, but something was preventing her from taking the
necessary action to earn her a promotion and she was beginning to
get frustrated.

When asked what was stopping her, she was stumped. 'I've no idea why I can't take the next step. I really want this pay rise but I just can't get started with what I know I need to do to get it.'

When asked what she would do with the extra money that would come with promotion, Angela hesitated and then said she'd buy a new car, but then she decided that wasn't her top priority. She thought about holidays, but couldn't imagine any holiday that would be facilitated by extra money. Angela liked shopping but couldn't imagine doing much more of it than she already did. So why did she want a pay rise when it wouldn't actually make any difference to her everyday life?

When Angela examined her motivation for promotion and earning more money a little more closely, she concluded that she was more interested in learning something new and taking on some new challenges as a means to raising her profile within the organization than she was in the extra money. She was really looking to put herself in a position where she gained more recognition for her contribution than her current position afforded her.

Angela's main objective was to create a more satisfying and gratifying work schedule. The increased salary was actually an added bonus, but by focusing on the money as the most important factor of the promotion, she was hampering her own progress. She needed to change something, but with money as her key motivator she found it hard to progress. It transpired that money was actually a relatively low priority. What Angela wanted to change most was her satisfaction and enjoyment level at work.

By focusing on how to increase her enjoyment, a completely unexpected opportunity arose at work which Angela seized with both hands and, as a result of this opportunity, she achieved her pay rise almost without trying.

Avoid chasing the money

For Angela, the need for security wasn't the key motivator behind her desire to progress at work and neither was the desire to increase her disposable income, so her initial focus on securing a pay rise actually slowed her progress down. As soon as she uncovered the correct motivating factors for her current situation – the desire for a more challenging and enjoyable work schedule – she was back on the road to success.

Insight

Occasionally the reasons why we act in specific ways aren't always obvious. We may think we're trying to achieve a particular end when the real reason we do what we do is something completely different. To achieve the best results you should spend a little time exploring your motivations for specific actions and behaviours at the deepest level. When you know your true motivation you can check that your behaviours are consistent with what you are aiming to achieve.

Successful people make money. It's not that people who make money become successful, but that successful people attract money. They bring success to what they do.

Wayne Dyer, author

Financial security is a major motivator for many people, and more money usually means more security, which is never a bad thing. Yet, as a motivating factor in life, security can have its limitations. Once a certain level of security has been achieved, you may require another motivator to drive you on to further success.

Ongoing motivation to succeed is usually born from the enjoyment of what you do. When successful people are asked how they came to be successful, there is usually one common theme running through their answers – they will invariably tell you that they love what they do. Many of them are handsomely rewarded for their work, however; often a healthy income seems like an added bonus to them. What's really important is that they enjoy their chosen career path.

The following information helps to categorize attitudes to work and finance. There are:

1 *People who enjoy what they do, who are paid well and are happy with their careers.*
2 *People who enjoy what they do but don't regard themselves as being particularly well rewarded for it.*
3 *People who consider themselves well rewarded financially but who don't enjoy what they do.*

Which category do you fall into? Which category would you like to be in? Decide what your priorities are for your finances, your earnings and the way in which you generate these earnings. Once you have achieved financial security, you will have more options on how you choose to earn your income.

First things first – your needs for security

The first step to establishing financial security is to make sure that your income is greater than your expenditure. First you must list all your monthly expenses. If you're unsure what they are, keep a money diary (see example on page 168) for at least one week, and ideally one month, to see where the money goes. This figure is the minimum amount your income needs to cover.

Your needs for life

Once you've established what you need to cover your outgoings, you must decide what more you want out of life. If you were able to increase your income, by how much would you want to increase it? What would you do with the money? Your finances are no different from any other area of your life. With clear objectives and strong

Financial diary		Today's date:
Time	Item	Amount spent

incentives, you will be in the best position to make your dreams a reality. Decide now how much disposable income you'd like to have each month.

Insight

Financial planning is a good example of an area where people can limit their success by setting their sights too low. The ability to think big when it comes to money pays dividends so stretch your thinking here beyond your traditional limitations and aim high with your plans for what you'd like to achieve.

Current financial situation
Income of ...... – expenditure of ...... = disposable income of ......

Desired financial situation
Income of ...... – expenditure of ...... = disposable income of ......

Once you have analysed your spending with your financial diary, it's time to implement some strategies that will help you keep control of it. Use the following version of the financial diary to highlight where you can save some money and how much you can save.

Financial diary			Today's date:	
Time	Item	Amount spent	Economical alternative	Amount saved

GATHERING THE EVIDENCE

If you are looking to save money, writing down everything you spend can be a dramatic way to see how much you can save and where you can save it.

Insight

With all plans and projects, your success is directly related to the accuracy of your original research material. Be honest with your financial diary and record everything you spend. The more accurate your diary, the easier it will be to make the right changes with your financial planning.

Bob was in a good job and earning a decent income, but he had some debts from his days as a student. He had become accustomed to living off what he earned and ignoring his debts, but as he thought about how he wanted his life to progress now, he realized that he needed to change his attitude and get himself financially straight.

Bob kept his financial diary for 20 days. For ten days he simply noted down all that he spent and for ten days he came up with some alternative spending patterns. He was shocked to calculate the amount he was on course to spend per month on lunch, coffees, magazines and other daily and weekly 'incidentals'. By cutting back on some of these things he worked his monthly spend in this area down dramatically.

By using the amount saved each month to pay off his debts, Bob would have cleared the amount he owed in 17 months. So he set about doing exactly that.

Top tips

▶ When you have established what you need for your weekly spending, take this amount from the cash point (ATM) at the beginning of the week and use it to get you through the week. It's harder to part with real money than it is to spend money on a credit or debit card, so get used to having your outgoings pass through your hands as paper and coins.

▶ Do something useful with the money that you save. Pay off debts or save it for a minor purchase you really want or a major purchase for which you will need some money behind you. Check your figures regularly to see your debts coming down or your savings going up. The fact that you can see some progress is a great incentive to keep going.

What does the future hold?

Now you have taken the first steps towards financial security, this is a great time to begin thinking in a more long-term way than you might be used to with your finances. With what you earn today you need to consider how you want to live in the future, including considering how much money you'd like to save each month, and what type of savings will suit you best. Are you saving cash for a rainy day in a savings account or in a tax-free saving product like an ISA (Individual Savings Account)? Do you have a pension plan in operation? Would you like to invest, perhaps in shares or property? Thinking about these things isn't everyone's cup of tea, but it's more appealing to do it sooner when you have the options and the opportunity to do something about your situation, than later when your enthusiasm and your earning ability may be somewhat diminished.

SETTING YOUR FINANCIAL EXPECTATIONS

As you know all too well by now, what you aim for is what you will achieve. If you set out to simply cover your expenses, this is what you will achieve. Aim higher and you will achieve this and much more. As you become more affluent, you need to continually raise the bar on what you want from your financial situation. Begin by aiming to spend less than you earn. Then start saving. Set clear objectives for your earnings and your savings. Create a financial buffer with an amount that would cover your expenses if you didn't work for a month or two. Invest carefully with clear parameters on what returns you are looking for from these investments. Review your finances regularly and make sure that they are in the best shape possible. Continually update your expectations of yourself and your finances. Choose how much cash you want to keep to hand, decide what level of balance you'd like to see regularly in your current account and by how much you want to see your savings grow each month.

Top tips

Pay off all debts. As part of your financial considerations, you need to look at any debts you may have. Invariably, the interest carried on debt is greater than the interest paid on savings, so do yourself a favour and get back to financial equilibrium as soon as you can. Having some savings is psychologically positive but not quite so good if much of those savings are owed to someone else.

Shop around. Some people spend money to save time, and this is fine if you have the money, you don't mind spending it, and you need the time. Others spend time to save money. These days it is easy to shop around on the internet or over the phone and it doesn't take very long. One client, Tom, claimed that he was too busy working to shop around for a new television. He knew the TV he wanted and he knew where to get it. Being slightly cautious by nature, Tom also wanted to add a five-year guarantee when he bought his television. Tom knew the total price he was looking to spend on his brand new hi-tech television and guarantee. He was given a challenge to spend just 30 minutes checking online that he had found the best price. It actually took him just five minutes to find the same television with a five-year guarantee included as well as delivery to the door and installation for 40 per cent less. Quite a saving for five minutes' work. Needless to say, no matter how hard or how much he worked, he had never had a job that paid that well.

Ask an expert. If you really don't have the inclination to spend time researching how you can save money, ask someone else to do it for you. Start with asking your bank manager whether there are any measures you can take to tighten up your finances, or seek out a financial adviser who can give you advice on debt repayment and finding the best deal on your mortgage, savings and investments. Many advisers make their money on the products they work with so they won't cost you a penny, but an adviser could save you a fortune in the long run by finding better deals on debts and mortgages and by helping you to make your money work harder with targeted savings and investment plans. Seeking expert help does not mean handing the whole thing over to someone else; rather, it is a way to broaden your information base. Get as much advice as you can, do some of your own research on what the experts are telling you, and make the best decisions based on your long-term financial plan.

Put some life into money

Thinking about money and how you'd like to earn it, save it and spend it is an essential part of most people's lives. Yet the concept of money and figures isn't always enough to get you excited. This is why it is important to use your planning skills to see money in the context of the rest of your life and what you want to achieve. Your money objectives should reflect your career objectives, and you should be able to see clearly how achieving your money objectives will benefit you and enrich your life. Keeping the benefits clear in your mind will ensure that you are fully motivated to achieve your financial goals.

Here is a real-life example of how this works:

	1-month objectives	6-month objectives	12-month objectives
Finances	► Consolidate my current financial position with regard to earnings and savings	► Salary increase of 20% ► Reduce all unnecessary expenditure ► Open ISA or other tax-free savings product	► Further salary increase of 15% ► Full ISA investment for this year ► Open investment account *(Contd)*

Work & career	▶	Explore opportunities for promotion in my current position	▶	New position within my current company	▶	New job with new company
Family & friends	▶	Take my family on a weekend away	▶	Take my family on two separate week-long holidays ▶ Design and budget for our house extension	▶	Take my family on a two-week holiday to Florida ▶ House extension complete
Hobbies	▶	Buy new set of golf clubs	▶	Play golf regularly ▶ Re-establish my painting	▶	New room complete in house extension for my artwork

PUT MONEY IN CONTEXT

Never view money in isolation. Always think about how it will affect and enrich your life and the lives of those close to you.

Insight

In life there is lots to think about and plenty to do. Sometimes making decisions can become overwhelming. Every single decision you have to make is made easier if there is some context to each dilemma and this context comes from reminding yourself regularly of your short-, medium- and long-term objectives. Judge each situation by whether it is in line with these objectives or not and then say yes or no accordingly.

THE LAW OF POSITIVE ATTRACTION

This law centres on your beliefs and your attitudes to money. What you believe here will have an impact on your prosperity, so be careful how you let your thoughts run. If you believe that money is out there to be had, you will have it. Update your financial beliefs so that they are in line with the life of wealth and abundance that you deserve.

Top tips

▶ If you owe money, pay it back as soon as you can. Avoid sending late cheques with second-class stamps. Pay bills in good time with a positive attitude as you settle them. You are choosing to pay for these items so do it with good grace. View all necessary spending as an investment in a lucrative future.

▶ Be generous. Don't be frivolous but be generous. What goes around comes around – if you are tight with your money, others will be tight with you. Be generous and those around you will be too.

▶ Develop a positive attitude to money. You know how to earn it and you know how to save and invest it wisely. You will never be short of money.

Seven steps to success – shape up your finances

1 IMMEDIATE ACTION

Remove any fear surrounding money. Consider what would happen if you were to lose your main source of income. You will still be the same person with the same knowledge, skills and understanding. You will be able to move on to something else. Your view of money can be clouded by fear of not having enough of it. By considering the worst-case scenario and realizing that you will survive, you can remove this fear and free yourself to create the circumstances you need for success.

2 RING THE CHANGES

Make sure your attitude to money is the right one. Think positive and think big. Decide now what your financial future holds for you. How does it differ from your financial past?

3 PLAN OF ATTACK

Decide what needs to be different with your finances. Are you pursuing greater income, less expenditure, living a debt-free existence or generating increased disposable income?

4 PRIORITIZE

Decide the order in which you will tackle your financial objectives. Devise a progressive plan for each area and follow it through to completion. There is no need to fix everything at once. Approach your finances in an order that suits you, and give yourself enough time in each area to make the changes you need to make.

5 REVIEW

Keep an eye on how you are progressing with your plan. Once you start you will be surprised at the speed with which you make progress in this area, so you will need to reset your objectives regularly to take account of this quick progress.

6 REWARD YOURSELF

Many people's way of thinking about finances revolves around short-term versus long-term pleasure or gratification. Spenders get immediate satisfaction from the things they buy. Savers get pleasure from watching their money grow over time or from spending it at some point in the future. Aim to strike a balance between the short-term pleasures that money can bring, such as treats and rewards on a regular basis, and the long-term pleasure of living a life in which, by being organized with your finances, you can enjoy your future with the choices and options that being financially secure brings with it.

7 PASS ON THE PLEASURE

As you enjoy the financial security that you have created, help others to enjoy it too. Spend some money on those you love and you will be the one who benefits the most. The pleasure of giving will become a part of your life and you will ensure that you maintain the financial situation that allows you to continue living in this fashion.

SUMMARY, PRACTICAL ACTIONS AND COMMITMENT

Your financial situation is as much about your attitude as it is about actual cash. History does not dictate your success in this area and you can begin a new page in your financial story whenever you like. Be realistic about your current situation and decide what really matters to you with your money and how you want to live in the future. Establish what financial security means to you and then achieve it. Sketch out a life of financial abundance and all the pleasure it will bring with it for you and your family and friends. Update your financial beliefs and then live a life of financial freedom.

Chapter 8 is about shaping up your financial situation. Now you know:
- ▶ *how to earn what you are worth*
- ▶ *how to reduce your expenditure*
- ▶ *how to set your financial expectations.*

Your commitment is to regularly review your financial situation and ensure that you are achieving your full potential in this area. Keep updating your financial expectations to maintain your progress. Once you have set new goals, and achieved them, you will never return to your previous financial situation unless you decide this is the correct way forward for you.

New you checklist

At the end of Chapter 8 you will be able to complete the following checklist.

Tick each statement when you are satisfied with your progress in this area:

You know clearly what you would like to be
earning. ☐
You can formulate a plan to earn this amount. ☐
You know how to establish financial security. ☐
You understand how money fits into your life. ☐
You have a clear idea of how extra income can
enrich your life. ☐
Your values and beliefs support your financial
objectives. ☐

10 THINGS TO REMEMBER

1 *Think about why money matters to you.*

2 *Decide what you think you are worth.*

3 *Consider how much money you need and how much you want.*

4 *Decide whether to reduce expenditure, or increase income, or both.*

5 *Do not limit yourself or your potential when it comes to earning money.*

6 *Ensure financial security as quickly as possible.*

7 *Then focus on the exciting opportunities that money brings you.*

8 *Manage your finances actively and regularly.*

9 *Settle debts, cover expenses, enjoy surplus cash, invest wisely.*

10 *You are in charge of your financial situation.*

9

Fantastic relationships

In this chapter you will learn:
- *to value your most important relationships*
- *how to take charge of your relationships*
- *to see things from the viewpoint of others*
- *to manage relationships to your advantage.*

The secrets of successful interaction with others

Someone was once heard to utter, 'The world would be an easier place if it wasn't for other people.'

This chapter is about how you fit into the world, whom you choose to have around you and how they affect your mood, your outlook on life and your happiness. By the end of the chapter, you will understand how you can guarantee positive relationships whoever you are with, wherever you are, and whatever you are doing.

> *The better part of one's life consists of his friendships.*
>
> Abraham Lincoln

Having read to this point in the book, you will have a much deeper understanding of what you want and need in life, and your new, greater self-awareness will have shown you how you can take action to achieve the things you want. You now know yourself in a way that you never have in the past. Therefore, surely now all you need to do is simply put your plans into action and everything will come good.

Now is the time when you face the challenges posed by other people. Very few people choose to live in isolation. Most people have to deal with others on a regular basis. Some of the people you come across will be as self-aware as you are and will be working to their own plan. Dealing with these people is relatively straightforward as all you have to do is work out how you will interact to mutual advantage. The skills you have learned so far can be used to uncover the beliefs, values, mission statement and objectives of these people, and you will be well placed to form good relationships with them.

Others may not be so sure of where their lives are taking them but they will still hold strong beliefs and values and have their own priorities during the time you interact with them. Again you can use your skills to uncover what motivates these people, and use this to shape your relationships with them.

Insight

Successful interaction with others is one of *the* key skills when it comes to upgrading your life. The ability to deal with many different types of people successfully will bring with it great opportunities and provide access to achievements you simply couldn't manage by yourself.

Relationships you choose

Just as people look different in subtle ways or very dramatic ways, their view of the world and the way they behave can differ from you and your view of the world subtly or dramatically. Generally, you will be drawn towards those who are most similar to you in their beliefs, behaviours and views of what matters in life as you feel most comfortable when surrounded by like-minded individuals. These are the people you choose to have as friends, and these friendships may develop into something deeper and stronger with those with whom you have the most in common.

Energy-giving relationships

Write down the names of five people with whom you get on brilliantly:

1

2

3

4

5

What do you have in common with these people?

What values do you share with these people?

What beliefs do you hold that are similar?

What do you enjoy doing with these people?

How do you feel when you are with these people?

Relationships you don't choose

There are also those people with whom you perhaps wouldn't choose to associate yourself but with whom you are forced into regular contact because you work with them or find yourself in social situations with them. Sometimes, this kind of relationship can even exist with family members – just because you are related by blood doesn't mean you will see life in the same way and get along with your parents, siblings or relatives.

Relationships that are positive can make you feel great, nourish your soul and give you energy for life. Relationships that are more challenging can take up much of your mental time and space and can sap you of energy and enthusiasm. The key to successful relationships is to seek out more of those that nourish you and to limit the contact you have with those who drain your energy, or minimize the effects you allow these people to have upon you. To help you do this, it is useful to understand the undercurrents of your relationships a little more deeply.

Energy-sapping relationships

Write down the names of five people whom you find it awkward to get on with:

1

2

3

4

5

(Contd)

Why do you find it awkward to deal with these people? Which of your values do they transgress? Which parts of their belief system are at odds with your belief system? What aspects of these characters do you find most frustrating?

Find the positives. There will be some elements of dealing with these people that are positive. To discover what these are, analyse these relationships in the same way as you did your energy-giving relationships. What do you have in common with these people? What values do you share? What beliefs do you hold that are similar? What do you enjoy doing with these people?

Switching the balance

When you are absolutely clear about what makes some relationships positive for you and others negative, it becomes easier to deal with the negatives. If you take the time to analyse the beliefs, values, needs and priorities of other people, you will understand their motivation for their behaviour. Whether you agree with their view of the world or not, the more you understand it and understand how it differs from your view of the world, the easier it will be for you to make a decision on whether you simply don't want to associate with this person any longer, whether you'd like to seek out the things you do have in common and confine the relationship to these areas, or whether you'd like to embrace the differences and create a relationship in spite of them. In many cases, opposites attract and can lead to a lasting and close relationship. Being aware of what you have in common with others, or what you don't have in common with them, at the earliest possible stage will ensure that your relationships are on the right footing from the outset.

Updating your relationships

Circumstances change, people change, and everyone develops and evolves over time so it is important to make sure you review your relationships regularly. You already understand the importance of updating your beliefs, your priorities and even your wardrobe. Similarly, you must update the company you keep to guarantee that you are supported in your aims in life and also to make sure that the people you have relationships with get the support they need too. Stale relationships do not benefit anyone so you must work to keep your relationships fresh by communicating and doing more of the things you enjoy together. At any time you may wish to change the dynamics of a relationship by altering the frequency with which you see someone or the circumstances under which you meet them. Be aware that if you set out to change the dynamics of a relationship, the other person must be happy with the changes. If they are not, they will resist and try to keep the relationship on the same footing, which may lead to tension.

Insight

Clear communication is vital when updating your relationships. Explain to the other person how you would like the relationship to change. Give reasons behind your thinking and make sure they are honest reasons. Update relationships only when you want them to move to a new footing. If you'd rather a relationship came to an end, you need to tackle this honestly too.

Relationships and compromise

Good relationships are easy. They are enjoyable and you rarely feel like you have to put much effort into them. Some relationships will require a little effort and with some you may wonder if they are even worth the trouble. If a relationship feels like a struggle, you have to decide whether or not you want to continue with it.

If you decide that it is worth continuing, you must adjust your expectations to avoid frustration in the future. There may be a certain amount of compromise required, but as long as you are aware of this as a general feature of the relationship, you will be best positioned to navigate your way through the ups and downs.

Real life, real people

CASE STUDY

Max had a group of friends he had been close to for a number of years. As they all got older and busier, they began to meet up less frequently as a group but he continued to see them all regularly, one or two at a time. They all kept in regular contact apart from one of the group who never called Max. They did see each other for drinks and the occasional meal but only if Max picked up the phone to organize these meetings, though even then it might be some time before his friend returned a voicemail or a text message to finalize the details of their engagement.

The situation began to frustrate Max, particularly as he and his friend had such a good time when they went out together. His friend always apologized for being poor at keeping in touch and vowed to be more diligent in the future but then always reverted to the same behaviour.

Max was getting to the stage where he wanted to stop calling his friend as he was fed up with doing all the running for the relationship. He pondered why he hadn't given up already and concluded that he really enjoyed the time they did spend together and he would feel a loss if he couldn't have that anymore. Increasingly though, the enjoyment was tinged with resentment that his friend never made any effort to arrange the meetings; he just arrived, had a good time and left.

Max was on the verge of ending a long-standing relationship. However, before he did so, there were some key questions for him to consider about his expectations of this relationship and whether or not he would be able to change his viewpoint and behaviour in any way that would make the relationship work better for him.

Managing your relationship expectations

- ▶ What are the positives of the current situation?

- ▶ What are the negatives of this situation?

- ▶ What can you control in this situation?

- ▶ What can't you control?

- ▶ What compromise could you make in this situation to improve it?

- ▶ Are you willing to make this compromise?

- ▶ What are the benefits of changing your expectations in this situation?

By altering his expectations of the friendship, Max was able to maintain it and continue to benefit from the positives of the interaction with this friend without the negatives of the resentment of the other person not making enough effort. He decided that the value of the relationship was high enough for him to accept that he was the one who kept it going. Knowing and accepting this allowed Max to enjoy the relationship again.

> **Insight**
> Good relationships, like anything in life, are dependent upon you getting the best out of the situation. To make sure you do get the best out of any situation you need to plan what you expect in advance. If you are clear on the best possible outcome and the worst possible outcome and all possibilities in between, for everything you do, you'll be in a great position to make educated judgements on how you spend your time.

Dealing with difficult people

So, there are some relationships that require compromise and careful management of your expectations to allow them to run smoothly. Other relationships may be more complex, and there will be people in your life whom you simply don't see eye to eye with. You might not share their beliefs or values or priorities or objectives but, for one reason or another, you need to get along with them. For these relationships, there is a coaching technique that you can employ to make sure that you get the best results for all concerned.

In any given circumstances in your life, you look out at the world through your eyes and listen with your ears, and what you see and hear and what you feel in a situation will be filtered and judged by your experience and by your beliefs and values. The same is true of those you are dealing with and, if your respective views of the world differ, you may disagree. If your views of the world differ drastically, then you may disagree dramatically.

When you come across other people's views of the world, you can open your mind to their perspective and accommodate their views, or you may disagree with their views and either keep quiet about it, or you may decide to express your own position more strongly. Until you are ready to update your beliefs, you will defend those you hold quite vigorously. It is when you come across people defending their beliefs that they can appear difficult. Whether they are being difficult or not is open to interpretation. After all, if those people were to deal with others who share their beliefs and worldview, they would not be seen as difficult. People are only seen as difficult when their worldviews are not in line with those with whom they are interacting at the time.

When you are in a situation with someone whose views don't match yours, things can become heated. You can probably remember a time when you got into an argument with someone because they wouldn't see things 'your way'.

When you are emotionally involved in a situation, the smallest issues can seem like the end of the world. When you get too deeply involved, you can sometimes lose perspective on a situation. The coaching technique of adopting different viewpoints on a situation will ensure that you keep things in perspective and will help you get to grips with who, if anyone, is being 'difficult'. It will also help you to overcome any difficulties and reach a workable solution.

CHANGING PERSPECTIVES

As you sit and read this book, move your focus from the words on the page and become aware of the situation you are in and the things around you. The chair you are sitting on, the floor, the walls, the colours, the furniture and the decoration. Imagine you are standing elsewhere in the room looking at yourself sitting reading. How does this notion change how you feel about what you are doing?

Now imagine you move outside the room so you are in effect observing yourself inside the room looking at yourself reading in the chair. How does this notion change how you feel about what you are doing?

First position – seeing the world through your own eyes

Second position – viewing a situation through the eyes of another

Third position – seeing a situation through the eyes of a third-party observer

The overview.

The bigger picture.

Imagine you are in a helicopter flying over your garden. You can see yourself looking in the window watching yourself standing in the room looking at yourself reading. How does this notion change how you feel about what you are doing?

As you take up vantage points progressively further away from the present moment viewed through your own eyes, you will find that the emotion of the moment is reduced and you increase your perspective of how what you are doing in the moment fits into the wider world. Changing perspectives helps you to put things in context and make judgements with a slightly more objective mindset. This can be an invaluable skill when making important decisions and particularly when interacting with others. Employing this technique will help you to remove tension from heated discussions. Forget for a moment how you see the situation and consider how the other person is viewing it. Think about how a third party would observe what's going on. What would someone who just entered the room to this scene think about what's going on? Whether it be an argument with a loved one, a disagreement with a friend or a debate with a work colleague, altering the viewpoint from which you see the situation will enable you to see the bigger picture, assess what needs doing from a fresh angle, and steer the moment to a more positive conclusion.

Changing the position from which you see a situation is a very effective way of putting yourself into the shoes of others and understanding where they may be coming from with their point of view. It's a powerful negotiating technique and a great way for you to perfect your argument in any situation. It's also a method of diffusing emotion. If you continually inhabit your own viewpoint – first position – you can become overly concerned with how each situation affects you, and not always in a good way. Imagining how others will see you, and how a third party would view the overall situation, will enable you to put yourself in context and consider whether the concerns that you have are in proportion to the situation and to your life as a whole. Experiment with this technique to rise above your immediate situation and get a new perspective on what is happening to you at any given time.

Insight

Distancing yourself in space or time helps you to make more considered decisions. It removes some of the emotion from situations. As well as changing the perspective from which you view a situation, experiment also with changing your view of time. Ask yourself, 'How will I feel about this decision/situation in one month, one year or even five years?' Think about how your response to this question affects your view of what's happening right now.

Position and performance

▶ Think of a discussion or meeting that you had, or presentation that you did recently.

▶ Rate yourself out of ten for how satisfied you were with your performance.

▶ How did you want to come across to the others in the room?

▶ Put yourself in their seat. How do you think you came across?

▶ If you had been a fly on the wall, what would you have thought of your performance?

▶ How does this information affect your future meetings? What will you do differently?

▶ Adopting different viewpoints will help you in any situation. Find examples of when you can next employ the technique, both at work and at home.

The next time I can try this technique at work is:

The next time I can try this technique at home is:

Susan was a very successful management consultant looking to take on a new challenge. She conducted careful research into the companies she would like to work for, sent out her CV and began to attend interviews. She was diligent with practising her presentation for these interviews but was concerned that she was thrown by a couple of obscure questions in her first interview. She had been caught off guard and felt that she had begun to ramble and talk too quickly which made her, in her opinion, appear scatty and disorganized.

Susan experimented with changing her viewpoint while she was rehearsing for her meetings. Instead of focusing on how the meeting would run when viewed through her own eyes, she thought about how her presentation would look when viewed through the eyes of those conducting the interview. She was now able to imagine what her presentation sounded like to the interviewers as new information being absorbed for the first time rather than a well-rehearsed sales pitch that she had practised repeatedly. This immediately helped Susan to anticipate the questions the others would ask.

Another concern Susan had about her interview technique was that, no matter how much preparation she did, when she arrived in the interview room, she got so caught up in the moment and by her surroundings that much of her preparation was forgotten. Also, when she was asked questions on particular topics, she felt that she got too involved in each topic, lost the thread of the interview and ended up talking off the point. This, she felt, made her come across with slightly less than the calm, professional image she wished to project.

Susan practised taking a mental step back from the immediate events to assess her performance in the interview as a whole rather than getting caught up in the heat of specific questions and answers. She implemented this by taking a physical step back at the beginning of each interview.

(Contd)

Every time she enters a room for a presentation, before she sits down, Susan takes a small step backwards. Unnoticeable to others, this step back is Susan's reminder to consider the situation she is in as a bigger picture event, and not to get too drawn in to the immediate preoccupations in her head. As an added back-up strategy, Susan also worked to associate sipping water, which she always did in interviews, with taking this mental step back. Now, every time she has a drink in a meeting, she is reminded to think about the detail of what she is saying, how the others will receive this information and how each interaction will affect the meeting as a whole and her objectives for it.

Seven steps to success – fantastic relationships

1 IMMEDIATE ACTION

If you are currently unhappy with someone, write down all the things that you're dissatisfied with. Put the list to one side and revisit it later when you have had a chance to calm down. Make sure that what you have written on your list is actually true and that you're not suffering from exaggeration to prove your own point or to fit in with what you want to believe. When you are calm, write down the truth of the situation, what your objective is in tackling it, and how best you can sort it out.

2 RING THE CHANGES

Reframe awkward situations and look for the positives. Disagreements may feel uncomfortable but your relationships cannot grow without them. You are unlikely to agree with everyone you know on every subject, so choose to view the differences as a way for everyone involved to gain new knowledge and find the best way forward.

3 PLAN OF ATTACK

Resolve now to spend more time among people with whom you have a positive relationship and less time with those who drain your energy.

4 PRIORITIZE

Keep yourself high up the priority list. If you are not happy with a relationship, you are unlikely to be able to make the other party truly happy. Make sure your own beliefs, values and needs are always catered for in order to put yourself in the best position to make the most of all your relationships.

5 REVIEW

Assess your relationships and interactions with others by looking at them from first, second, third, fourth and fifth positions. How do you see the situation, how do they see the situation and how would a third party interpret it?

6 BE FLEXIBLE BUT FIRM

Be prepared to make compromises but make them on your own terms. As long as you still feel in control of a relationship, you will be content. If you feel you are being taken advantage of, establish where you can regain control and act swiftly.

7 BE GENEROUS IN YOUR RELATIONSHIPS

Remember what relationships are all about. We learn from each other, grow together and enhance each other's lives. Think about what you can give to others more than what you can get from them and you will have many rewarding relationships.

SUMMARY, PRACTICAL ACTIONS AND COMMITMENT

Fantastic relationships begin with your relationship with yourself. The happier you are, the happier you will be able to make other people. This is possible because happy and fulfilled people are able to interact with others without agenda, pretence or malice. Use the techniques in the book to raise your self-awareness and to get what you want in your life. Then share the benefits of this with others.

Spend time and enjoy those who share your beliefs, values and view of the world. Use your knowledge in these areas to enhance your relationships with those who hold slightly different views.

> Chapter 9 is about how you relate to others. Now you know:
>
> ▶ *how to seek out relationships that nourish you*
> ▶ *how to maximize the benefits of your positive relationships*
> ▶ *how to minimize the negative effects of relationships that challenge you.*

Your commitment is to be selective with how you choose to manage your relationships. Make sure they are mutually beneficial at all times, and if you feel the balance has gone from a relationship, take the appropriate action to reconcile the situation sooner rather than later.

New you checklist

At the end of Chapter 9 you will be able to complete the following checklist.

Tick each statement when you are satisfied with your progress in this area:

You understand the essence of positive relationships.	☐
You know what makes some relationships negative.	☐
You are able to spend more time in positive relationships.	☐
You understand the importance of updating your relationships.	☐
You know how to keep control of your relationships.	☐
You can manage your expectations in relationships.	☐
You understand how to take first, second, third, fourth and fifth positions.	☐
You can use these viewpoints to your advantage.	☐

10 THINGS TO REMEMBER

1 *Your relationships hold the key to fast-track success in many areas of life.*

2 *The better you know yourself, the stronger your relationships with others will be.*

3 *Choose who you spend time with carefully.*

4 *Update your social circle regularly.*

5 *Seek out people who will nourish you and help you develop.*

6 *Seek out people who will challenge you and help you evolve.*

7 *Communicate clearly with everyone you come into contact with.*

8 *View managing relationships as a skill to be practised.*

9 *In life you might have to spend time with people who wouldn't be top of your list of friends. Accept that you need to be able to manage these relationships well.*

10 *Examine what you can learn from every relationship and interaction you have with those around you.*

10

The new you – reaping the rewards

In this chapter you will learn:
- *how far you have come since the beginning of the book*
- *to acknowledge and enjoy your development through life*
- *the triumph of a life lived well.*

Celebrating your success

Congratulations on every single change you have made to your life so far. You now have a very different outlook than when you began this book and you will now be able to feel positivity and personal power flowing through you at all times. With your new skills and strategies, you will have the confidence to deal with every situation you come across and work towards the outcome that benefits you most.

You now have the ability to take your life in any direction you want and it is your duty to do just that. Seek out opportunities to put the new you into action. Test yourself regularly to see what you are capable of. Challenge yourself to take some risks and never stop learning. There is no right or wrong in what you do as long as you continue to grow and develop every day. Be curious and take nothing for granted. Question everything until you understand what works for you.

As well as continuing your self-development, it is important to recognize and acknowledge how far you have come. This is crucial because it will ensure that you are always aware of your great achievements, and you can learn from them and use the successful strategies that you have created again and again with future challenges. Maintaining an awareness of your own successes will keep your confidence high. When you examine the challenges that you've overcome, you will know that you can deal with anything that life sends your way.

You must also celebrate your success. The efforts you make to instigate change will be reward in themselves as the quality of your day-to-day life continually improves. It is also important to formally reward yourself along the way because an added incentive here and there will see you through the toughest of times. Your rewards can be whatever you choose, ranging from giving yourself a day off or treating yourself to a massage to taking yourself off for a special day out or simply relaxing in the bath. All that matters is that you include plenty of rewards and incentives in your schedule, and frequently enough for you to say thank you to yourself for a job well done.

> *The moment of victory is much too short to live for that and nothing else.*
>
> Martina Navratilova

All that remains now is for you to look back to the objectives you set yourself in the introduction and see how you have performed in relation to what you wrote at that time.

▶ What have you learned since the beginning of this book?

▶ What has been your greatest achievement?

▶ What has changed?

- ▶ What has been the greatest benefit to you of these changes?

- ▶ What's your next big exciting challenge?

- ▶ What areas would you like to do more work on?

- ▶ How will you celebrate your success so far?

> *The biggest adventure you can ever take is to live the life of your dreams.*
>
> Oprah Winfrey

The world and your role in it change continually. At times, you will feel ahead of the game. At other times you will feel discomfort and ready for further development. Embrace all parts of the process and enjoy them equally. Revel in your triumphs and acknowledge any discomfort as a sign that some work needs to be done. Your new skills will enable you to pinpoint where to focus your attentions and put in the effort to move forward. Life is full of ups and downs and is an ongoing process of growth and renewal. Sometimes you will be in complete control, and at other times you may need to minimize your risk and then take a leap of faith. Stay focused on what you want to achieve and maintain faith in yourself and you will be handsomely rewarded for your efforts.

Real life, real people

Keeping the faith

Kate had been working in the media since she left university. Having spent her early career doing everything and anything to learn as much as she could about her industry, she achieved a high-level executive position that she loved. The hours were long and her role and the company she worked for were very demanding, but Kate was thriving in an environment where she was busy, productive and well respected for her opinions and the results she achieved.

After three years in this position, Kate decided it was time to move on. She was still pleased with her performance in her current role but she was also aware of the danger of the relentless pressure and how it might begin to take a toll on her if it were to continue. She also liked the idea of moving to a different arena where there would be new challenges and, ideally, a little less pressure. At the level Kate had reached in her company, there weren't that many new jobs to choose from and it soon became apparent that there was a decision to be made between choosing a job that would be enjoyable but probably not excessively challenging, and hanging on for a role that would really push her on to greater heights.

Although Kate had been very successful in her career so far, there was one thing missing from her personal skill set, and that was confidence. Ever since she could remember, she had suffered from a lack of confidence in her ability. Everyone she encountered in her working life could see what a natural talent Kate had for her job and how passionate she was about her industry, many of them even commented to her about this but, because these things came naturally to Kate, she didn't think anything of them or even rate these features of her personality as attributes. She simply did what she did at work because she believed in it and never thought of herself as anything special. Worse than that, Kate was so unsure of herself that she often felt like she wasn't up to the job and felt concerned that others might feel the same. Often she lived in fear that she would be uncovered as a 'fake' and that would be the end of her career.

Plagued by this lack of confidence, Kate chose a new role within the company that she knew would be well within her capabilities and her professional comfort zone.

(Contd)

The new position worked out well initially and was certainly less pressured than Kate's previous job. This was fine to begin with but, as the novelty of having more time to complete tasks wore off, Kate grew restless. Having more time on her hands actually became damaging as it gave her less confident side freedom to roam. She began to analyse everything she was doing and worried about whether it was perfect or not. Whereas before she would have completed a project and then moved quickly on to the next, now she had time to continually reassess decisions and often ended up undoing much of her own good work.

In her new role, Kate had less autonomy than in her previous position, and she found this very frustrating. Much of the enjoyment that she experienced at work came from being creative and having the freedom to explore new ideas and work them into completed projects. She no longer had the scope to do this, and as time went by, the situation became quite damaging for Kate. Because the job didn't allow her to do much of what she really enjoyed, she became less and less confident in her ability to do anything well.

When Kate reached her lowest ebb, she sought help with some coaching. She had lost all faith in her career, was upset at the choice she had made when changing jobs, and now felt incapable of finding another position. She felt as though her career had peaked and she was disheartened that she'd been too busy to notice or acknowledge how well things had been going previously. Now she didn't know what she was going to do next.

The first thing for Kate to do was to put to rest any regret she felt about her previous decision to change jobs. Beating herself up about past decisions was simply unproductive. Instead, she was encouraged to examine everything that was positive about what had happened and focus on what she would do differently if the situation were ever to be repeated.

The first positive thing that Kate acknowledged was the many aspects of her previous role that she had enjoyed. It hadn't been perfect but she now could acknowledge that it was important for her to face tough challenges each day, to feel like she was constantly learning something new, and that she was appreciated and liked among her colleagues. She also now recognized that not everyone could have carried out the role that she did and that maybe she did have some talent after all.

Next, Kate explored why she was so frustrated in her current position and why she had lost her confidence even further. When she looked at what was working in her current role, Kate realized that she actually had a 100 per cent success rate with the projects that she worked on. She also felt excited and energized when she worked on these projects. The problem was that these projects were few and far between so that all the success and the positive feelings attached to them were overshadowed by the frustration she felt for the majority of her working day. Kate now accepted that it wasn't the case that she was poor at her job, quite the opposite in fact. The problem was that she was very rarely given the opportunity to do her job – to do what she loved and what gave her the greatest sense of satisfaction.

Gradually, by assessing her situation from the outside, Kate managed to generate a little self-confidence. In the beginning, she felt it was a great effort and that she was faking the confidence, but she was aware that it was important to make this approach work as something new and different in her life. She knew that she couldn't go on as she was, living through daily frustration at work, because it was beginning to seriously affect her outlook on life.

Kate wrote down everything she loved about the work she had done over the years. She also wrote down all the aspects of work that she didn't like and that she needed to avoid in her next position. She then put the word out that she was looking for a new position. Within a single week, she had received four offers from people who wanted her to work with them. All the offers were attractive but three of them contained just too many aspects from the list of things Kate wanted to avoid. The fourth role didn't seem
(Contd)

ideal at first but only because it was a big challenge. Her overriding thought was: what if she wasn't up to it?

Kate's lack of confidence was haunting her again so she returned to look at the evidence in front of her. During the period that she now viewed as the time her career 'peaked', she was working out of her comfort zone for much of the time. With hindsight she could see that she had been so busy she didn't have time to worry about not being confident in what she did – she just had to get on with it. In her recent role, her inactivity had caused her to plumb the depths of despair. Now she had an opportunity to jump to something exciting, but she was hesitating. She was holding herself back.

Kate considered the question 'What would be the one thing that would enable me to feel better with the decision of taking this challenging role?' Her answer to this was 'Knowing that it would be the right decision.' Kate's biggest regret was that she had allowed her lack of confidence to push her towards a lesser challenge when leaving her previous position. The result was that her inactivity had chipped away at her confidence even further. She resolved never to make that mistake again and decided that the only way to find out if taking the challenging new role was the right decision would be to say yes to it. Downshifting her career had not been a positive experience for her so now she decided she would commit to testing herself a little harder. To minimize her risk she asked herself 'What's the worst that could happen?' and concluded that whatever course things took from here, it would be better than her current situation.

Kate accepted the new role and is thriving on it. She now feels she has regained the direction in her career and is growing in confidence with every new project she has to research and every decision she has to make. There's not much time for self-doubt as there are too many other things to be getting on with.

When asked what she had learned from this tricky period, Kate replied: 'I wish I had been better at taking a step back from my own situation and could have seen what was actually going on rather than getting stuck in my own interpretation of everything around me. If I could have done that, I would have realized that I created and perpetuated my lack of confidence by putting myself in situations where things could only get worse. I'm really pleased to have been able to change that pattern and realize now that certain tasks shouldn't scare me – in fact it's the scary things that bring me the most positive experiences. Above all, I wish I'd had more faith in myself and my abilities.'

Kate's experience is one that anyone might go through – sometimes, it can be difficult to see a way forward when caught in the middle of such an experience. Now, with your ability to coach yourself to success with whatever challenges you take on in life, you can maintain a clear head and the right attitude to face these challenges head on. Establish what you need to do and take action to put yourself where you want to be quickly and easily, and enjoy the journey as you make it.

Use this book to help you through the challenges of life. Revisit the exercises whenever you feel you could benefit from new perspectives and insights with issues you are facing. The work you do will ensure you succeed, so remember to enjoy and appreciate your development along the way.

All the very best for the future.

> *Live all you can – it's a mistake not to. It doesn't so much matter what you do in particular, so long as you have your life. If you haven't had that, what have you had?*
>
> Henry James

Taking it further

If you would like further advice on living the life you have always dreamed of, visit www.upgrade-my-life.com or contact one of our expert coaches on 020 8995 9927.

Other resources for specialist coaching advice

The Life Coaching Academy
www.lifecoachingacademy.com

The International Coach Federation
www.coachfederation.org.uk

Association for Coaching
www.associationforcoaching.com

Further reading and website resources

The 7 Habits of Highly Effective People, Stephen R. Covey
www.stephencovey.com

42 Days to Wealth, Health and Happiness, Robin Sieger
www.siegerinternational.com

Awaken the Giant Within, Anthony Robbins
www.anthonyrobbins.com

Feel the Fear and Do It Anyway, Susan Jeffers
www.susanjeffers.com

Introduction to NLP, John Seymour
www.john-seymour-associates.co.uk

Instant Confidence, Paul McKenna
www.paulmckenna.com

Life DIY, Pete Cohen
www.sortyourlifeout.com

FURTHER ONLINE RESOURCES

For a great daily motivational quote newsletter and much more, go to www.self-growth.com

For a weekly inspirational postcard, sign up for Victoria Lim Gems at www.veronicalim.com

Practical coaching advice available at www.creatingpower.com

Useful financial advice can be had from The Motley Fool at www.fool.co.uk

To find an independent financial adviser, visit www.unbiased.co.uk and www.adviceonline.co.uk

---

Training resources

If you would like to pursue a career in coaching, you may contact:

The Life Coaching Academy
www.lifecoachingacademy.com

If you have a particular interest in Neuro Linguistic Programming (NLP) and its application to coaching contact:

John Seymour Associates
www.johnseymourassociates.co.uk

The Performance Partnership
www.performancepartnership.com

Appendices

Here you will find blank copies of key exercises and questions that can be revisited at any time of your life. To stay on track and be as effective as you possibly can be at all times, aim to review your progress regularly and continue working towards your ideal life each and every day.

Appendix 1

DAILY LEARNING JOURNAL

Use your journal to review each day and re-orientate your plans, objectives, thoughts and tasks for tomorrow.

Daily journal

Today's date:

What did I enjoy doing today?

What would I like to do more of?

What would I like to do less of?

What did I learn today?

What will I do differently tomorrow?

Thought for the day

Appendix 2

Use the lifestyle rating questionnaire at regular intervals to review your current priorities for change.

	Dissatisfied									Fully satisfied
Confidence levels	0 1 2 3 4 5 6 7 8 9 10
Personal relationships	0 1 2 3 4 5 6 7 8 9 10
Family life	0 1 2 3 4 5 6 7 8 9 10
Friends	0 1 2 3 4 5 6 7 8 9 10
Effectiveness at home	0 1 2 3 4 5 6 7 8 9 10
Energy levels	0 1 2 3 4 5 6 7 8 9 10
Fitness	0 1 2 3 4 5 6 7 8 9 10
Stamina	0 1 2 3 4 5 6 7 8 9 10
Nutrition habits	0 1 2 3 4 5 6 7 8 9 10
Body shape	0 1 2 3 4 5 6 7 8 9 10
Physical appearance	0 1 2 3 4 5 6 7 8 9 10
Career development	0 1 2 3 4 5 6 7 8 9 10
Financial situation	0 1 2 3 4 5 6 7 8 9 10
Ability to cope with stress	0 1 2 3 4 5 6 7 8 9 10
Effectiveness at work	0 1 2 3 4 5 6 7 8 9 10
Enjoyment of your leisure time	0 1 2 3 4 5 6 7 8 9 10
Ability to manage your time	0 1 2 3 4 5 6 7 8 9 10
Ability to prioritize	0 1 2 3 4 5 6 7 8 9 10
Personal development	0 1 2 3 4 5 6 7 8 9 10
Ability to balance your life	0 1 2 3 4 5 6 7 8 9 10
Happiness	0 1 2 3 4 5 6 7 8 9 10
Overall satisfaction with life	0 1 2 3 4 5 6 7 8 9 10

Appendix 3

Answer the following questions regularly to focus your action and raise your scores for the lifestyle ratings questionnaire quickly.

Instant progress questions

1 What would have to happen in this area of my life for me to be able to score myself higher?

2 What would I like my rating out of ten to be in this area?

3 By what date could I improve my rating in this area?

4 What's the first action I need to take to begin raising my score in this area of my life?

5 When can I take this first action?

Appendix 4

Use the following template to plan in detail every change that you're going to make in your life.

> # Key factors for successful change
>
> ▶ A clear objective
>
>   What are you setting out to achieve?
>
> ▶ Research
>
>   What do you need to know to achieve your objective?
>
> ▶ Action
>
>   What do you need to do?
>
> ▶ Accountability
>
>   In addition to yourself, who are you going to make yourself responsible to?
>
> ▶ Structure
>
>   Outline the progressive sequence of your actions towards your objective.
>
> *(Contd)*

▶ Feedback, flexibility and modification

Consider all the aspects of your plan that you don't have full control over.
Consider some contingency plans to keep you on track towards your objective in the face of new events and learning.

▶ End point

How will you know when you've achieved success? Describe what your life is like at this point.

Appendix 5

You are continually developing and the world is constantly changing. Use the following questions to ensure you are always living the life you desire.

Uncovering personal motivation 1 – what do you really want?.

▶ If you could have anything in life, what would you have?

▶ If you were living your ideal life, what would you be doing
  ▷ every day?

  ▷ every week?

  ▷ every month?

  ▷ every year?

▶ What does success mean to you? Not to society or to your friends, family or those around you, but what does it mean to you? What would be *your* greatest success in life?

▶ What single thing would make you truly happy?

▶ If you were to live your life again, knowing what you know now, what would you do differently?

Appendix 6

It is important to keep your values, your life purpose and your mission statement up to date. You can do this by keeping the following information up to date.

Uncovering personal motivation 2 – why you want what you want

Think about what is currently important in your life

▶ Why do I enjoy doing these things?

▶ What does doing these things do for me or get for me?

▶ How does doing these things enhance my life?

▶ What's really important about doing these things in my life?

▶ How would I feel if I couldn't do these things in my life?

My current mission statement

Appendix 7

Your beliefs evolve through life. Check them regularly to ensure that they support you in all your aims in life.

> ## The power of beliefs
>
> Highlight five of your own current and supportive beliefs.
>
> 1   I believe...
>
> 2   I believe...
>
> 3   I believe...
>
> 4   I believe...
>
> 5   I believe...

Appendix 8

Update your life planner regularly to ensure that your objectives are still current, relevant and exciting.

Planner

Setting your objectives – what do you most want to achieve in life?
Today's date:

Work and career
- ▶ 4-week objectives
- ▶ 6-month objectives
- ▶ 18-month objectives

Health, fitness, food, well-being
- ▶ 4-week objectives
- ▶ 6-month objectives
- ▶ 18-month objectives

Hobbies, social, fun, relaxation
- ▶ 4-week objectives
- ▶ 6-month objectives
- ▶ 18-month objectives

Partner, family and friends
- ▶ 4-week objectives
- ▶ 6-month objectives
- ▶ 18-month objectives

Finances
- ▶ 4-week objectives
- ▶ 6-month objectives
- ▶ 18-month objectives

Appendix 9

Use these questions regularly to ensure your objectives are always irresistible.

> ### Visualizing success – what's in it for you?
>
> **When you reach your objective, how will you feel?**
>
> Confident? Self-satisfied? Triumphant? Powerful? Happy?
>
> **When you reach your objective, how will life be different?**
>
> Imagine that you have just achieved your objective and consider how life now changes for you.
>
> **When you reach your objective, what does your day look like? What activities does your day contain?**
>
> **When you reach your objective, what activities will you no longer have to put up with? Of the tasks on your current daily to-do lists, what will you be able to remove?**
>
> **When you reach your objective, what will others be saying about you?**
>
> *(Contd)*

When you reach your objective, what do you say to others about yourself?

How does achieving your objective affect your self-image and the image you portray to those around you?

Is your vision of reaching your objective exciting enough to encourage you to take instant action?

What instant action will you take?

Appendix 10

As your life develops, so will your thoughts on people you admire.
Update your role models regularly.

List five people that you would like to use as role models and
note down what it is about their character or their life that you
admire and aspire to.

Role model 1
What is it about this person that inspires me?

Role model 2
What is it about this person that inspires me?

Role model 3
What is it about this person that inspires me?

Role model 4
What is it about this person that inspires me?

Role model 5
What is it about this person that inspires me?

Index

Notes

Notes

Notes

Notes

Notes

Notes

Notes

Notes

Notes

Notes

Image credits